1968

STATE LIBRARY
REGIONAL CENTER
CALDWELL, OHIO

Mexico's Magic Square

Other Books of Travel and Adventure
by Erle Stanley Gardner

OFF THE BEATEN TRACK IN BAJA
GYPSY DAYS ON THE DELTA
HUNTING LOST MINES BY HELICOPTER
THE WORLD OF WATER
THE DESERT IS YOURS
THE HIDDEN HEART OF BAJA
HOVERING OVER BAJA
HUNTING THE DESERT WHALE
NEIGHBORHOOD FRONTIERS
THE LAND OF SHORTER SHADOWS

MEXICO'S

MAGIC SQUARE

by Erle Stanley Gardner

WILLIAM MORROW & COMPANY, INC.

NEW YORK 1968

Copyright © 1968 by Erle Stanley Gardner

All rights reserved. No part of this book may be reproduced or utilized in any form or by any means, electronic or mechanical, including photocopying, recording or by any information storage and retrieval system, without permission in writing from the Publisher. Inquiries should be addressed to William Morrow and Company, Inc., 425 Park Avenue South, New York, N.Y. 10016.

Published simultaneously in Canada by George J. McLeod Limited, Toronto.⎯

Printed in the United States of America.

Library of Congress Catalog Card Number 68-30865

Contents

Color photographs follow page 58

List of Illustrations

Mexico's Magic Square

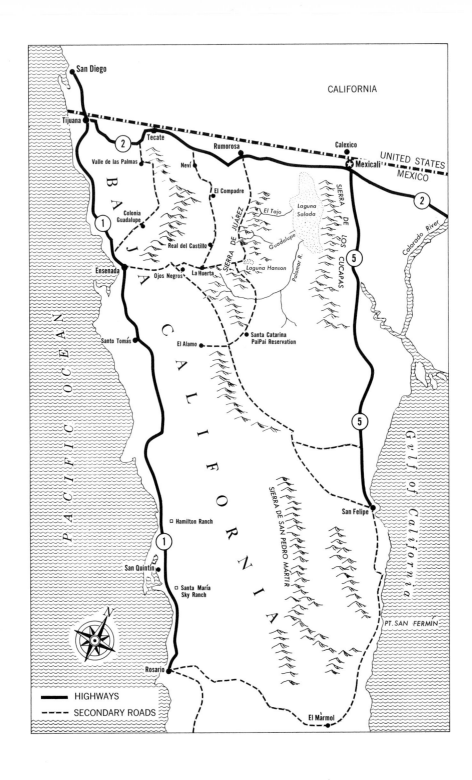

1

Mexico's Magic Square

For many years I explored Mexico's Baja California by the so-called main road. I traversed the entire length of the peninsula and I knew intimately every foot of the dangerous road along the Bahía de la Concepción. I spent many days in Mulegé, San Ignacio, Santa Rosalía, and La Paz. And, by using helicopters, I covered the back country; yet I had only a hazy idea of that portion of the terrain lying immediately south of the border and within a hundred and fifty miles of the international boundary.

Upon making inquiries I found virtually no one knew exactly what was in this territory. Everyone knew, of course, of Tijuana, Ensenada, Mexicali, Tecate, and San Felipe; but what of the Sierra de Juárez, of the PaiPai Indians, of Laguna Salada?

This section of Mexico is so close it has apparently been overlooked by exploring tourists.

We are all familiar with what happened when Oklahoma was opened to settlers.

A crowd of people gathered at the boundary to wait for the starting signal. They had all sorts of transportation. Some

Exploring a canyon in Baja California by helicopter.

Weird shapes dot the landscape of Baja California.

A typical stretch of the thousand miles of dirt road in Baja California.

were riding the swiftest horses obtainable, ready at the sound of the gun to use whip and spurs, each rider trying to outdistance the other so as to get into the most choice lands in the virgin territory.

Came the sound of the starting signal and they were off, a vast horde of eager settlers galloping in one of the wildest horse races ever known—crowding, pushing, spurring, fighting to get ahead.

After the dust-covered line of horsemen had faded into the distance, a few of the really smart ones simply stepped across the line and staked out the choicest territory of all—land which everyone had overlooked in the mad desire to get ahead of all competition.

To some extent, that's the way it is in Baja California.

For years, people (myself included) have been "exploring" Baja California by using various four-wheel-drive vehicles and fighting their way down the long miles of dirt road.

In our eagerness to get over the thousand miles of road between Tijuana and Cabo San Lucas at the southern tip of the peninsula, we have—for the most part—overlooked the terrain which is closest to the United States, and which contains some of the most interesting country to be found in Baja California.

I confess that I discovered this country quite by accident. Having a fleet of four-wheel-drive cars and specially designed dune buggies, and having done a lot of exploring in chartered airplanes and helicopters, I fancied this part of Baja California was hardly worthy of a full-scale expedition.

How wrong I was!

Baja California is a land of wonders, a place of adventure. And Baja California starts immediately south of the border and stretches interminably to well below the Tropic of Cancer.

Variety of desert growth provides interesting scenery.

In some places the roads are quite good; in some places they are narrow, steep, dangerous, single-track roads clinging to the sides of precipitous mountains.

A motorist who comes to a detour of ten to fifteen miles of dirt road in the United States is dust covered and angry by the time he reaches the end of the detour.

Imagine a dirt detour stretching for some nine-hundred-odd miles, six hundred of it through dust and sand, over rocks, across mountains and desert under such conditions that the average caravan must consider sixty to seventy miles a really good day's travel. In fact, there are sections of the road where thirty to forty miles is a good day's quota. And I have been in some terrain where we were crossing a desert simply by compass course, and ten miles a day was all we could make.

Baja California is a peninsula, varying in width from around a hundred and fifty miles down to a narrow point of perhaps a little over thirty miles.

In places there are high mountains rising over ten thousand feet along the backbone of the peninsula. At other places there are great level expanses of desert jungle, a sandy soil simply choked with the huge cardon cactus, verde trees, the weird cirio trees, and the smaller cacti of the opuntia family—and the biznagas which, in turn, are overshadowed by the organ-pipe cactus.

Heaven knows how many varieties of cactus there are in the peninsula!

There is also the creeping-devil cactus—a huge worm-shaped affair covered with wicked spines, which actually crawls over the surface of the desert, clinging to the sand. The dirigible balloon-shaped tubes—growing and stretching out—are moving, always moving, across the sand.

At the northern end, the peninsula is perhaps a hundred and fifty miles wide in an air line. On the border at the ex-

An expanse of desert jungle.

Cacti in abundance.

Both roads cross rather high mountains.

treme west is Tijuana; then some thirty-one miles to the east is Tecate; after that, a hundred and fifteen road miles from Tijuana, one comes to the city of Mexicali.

Between these cities is a paved Mexican road south of the border, and a paved United States road north of the border. Both roads cross rather high mountains. Then the roads drop abruptly into the desert, the United States road into the Imperial Valley and the Mexican road into the grim desert of the Laguna Salada. The eastern slopes of the mountains are sheer. The western side gradually builds up in a series of foothills which rise higher and higher until they reach the crest, where one looks down from a dizzy height to the desert below.

On the Mexican side of the border this desert is a forbidding, barren, dangerous place where the sun beats down, sucking out moisture and leaving only shriveled, parched, stunted desert growth to fight for existence.

The Author piloting a "Butterfly" over the sand hills.

Our four-wheel-drive vehicles and the "Grasshopper," second from the right.

For years I had been exploring desert stretches—using four-wheel-drive automobiles, helicopters, and some of those weird contraptions invented by my friend J. W. Black, and which he had christened the Pak-Jak, the Burrito, the Butterfly and the Grasshopper.

I could write a chapter about the histories of these various vehicles and still not exhaust the subject. But at the moment I want to talk about how we became acquainted with the little-known PaiPai Indians, about the mysterious palm canyons which very few people have seen, the hot sulphur springs, the streams of flowing water in canyons which are supposed to be part of a parched desert, and various other things which the average tourist knows nothing about.

Later on we will move on to Tijuana, to Mexicali, to San Felipe and Ensenada, go on expeditions down the backbone of the Sierra de Juárez—the mountains which stretch between the ocean on the west and desert on the east.

At this time, suffice it to say that Tijuana is an intriguing, colorful Mexican city, far more complex than the two-dimensional picture which most travelers get in a hurried automobile visit across the border.

Only a few miles from San Diego, Tijuana offers an opportunity to the tourist to extend his journey from Los Angeles and San Diego over into Mexico.

Since he can reach Tijuana over the express paved highway in around half an hour from downtown San Diego, the automobile tourist is prone to include Tijuana as a side trip so he can add Mexico to the foreign countries he has visited.

It is unfortunate that Tijuana is so accessible and so near the border. It means the tourist who is in a hurry can have breakfast in Los Angeles, lunch in San Diego, make a quick trip down to Tijuana, and return to his hotel in Los Angeles late that evening.

Tijuana from the air.

Ensenada from the air.

This is really letting the tourist cheat himself out of the things he should see and the things he should do. It is bad for San Diego and it is bad for Tijuana, because the latter city has geared itself so largely to catering to tourists who drive in, look around in a few shops, and then drive out. If Tijuana were a little farther from the border, it might well have become a world-famous resort city.

The good things of Tijuana should be better known. The tourist should visit the better restaurants and stay overnight to get the unique atmosphere of the place, the joys of shopping in duty-free stores. And San Diego in itself is well worth a two-day visit. The sophisticated traveler knows that everything Southern California has to offer can be found in San Diego—climate, scenery, restaurants, Mission, historical background, year-around golf, fishing, good hotels; in short, everything.

Here again, however, there have been problems. For a while, the United States customs, trying to protect the merchants in San Diego, decreed that the Tijuana tourist could bring back only a scant ten dollars in purchases without paying duty.

Gradually the policy-making officials learned that this was a mistake. The more prosperous Tijuana becomes, the more prosperous San Diego is. So now customs regulations have changed and the tourist can bring back a hundred dollars of duty-free merchandise, provided he doesn't do this more frequently than once a month.

To the south of Tijuana is Ensenada, some sixty-five miles over a high-speed toll road which offers some of the most beautiful marine scenery in the world. Ensenada is a busy port and, as we shall presently see, has an atmosphere and charm which is a delightful balm to the tourist who can take the time to enjoy it.

On the east, Mexicali is even closer to the international

The International Border separating the twin cities.

border than is Tijuana. In fact, the twin cities of Calexico and Mexicali are nestled together so that only the international fence separates the two. Calexico for many years enjoyed the only really deluxe hotel at that part of the border—the De Anza Hotel, although there were several first-class motels.

Now, however, Mexicali has come up with a modern hotel, laid out on spacious grounds, with a swimming pool, protected patios, fountains, bar, coffee shop, dining room, and, in general, the facilities of a luxury hotel.

Recently Colonel José M. Gutiérrez took us on a trip of inspection through Mexicali and then took us to lunch at a new restaurant which is specializing in seafood, flown in from Veracruz.

Through my friend Lic. Ignacio Guajardo, we were able to have a chat with the manager of the Mexicali Chamber of Commerce, Ing. Aurelio Flores Valenzuela.

The swimming pool and patio of Mexicali's modern hotel, Lucerna.

Left to right: My friend, Colonel José M. Gutiérrez, and the manager of the Mexicali Chamber of Commerce, Ing. Aurelio Flores Valenzuela.

One of the beautifully designed houses in Mexicali.

The display window of a Mexicali curio store. Note reflections of the palm trees.

Mexicali has a population of some four hundred and eighty thousand, and, in addition to the CETYS University, has a branch of the University of Baja California—a state-supported university.

Raising cotton is the principal industry, but there are large canning factories which can vegetables and juices, and there is quite a business in tomatoes and vegetables.

Mexicali has some really beautiful homes. Some of the older houses show the typical Mexican architecture—graceful, winding stairways coupled with an outward appearance of substantial beauty. New city subdivisions are springing up with modern houses, but I personally love the older houses which are more typical of traditional Mexican architecture.

Mexicali, however, does not attract the number of tourists that Tijuana does; and in recent years Mexicali has grown into a dignified, bustling city with fine homes and good stores. It also is bursting at the seams with a population influx. For that matter, the same is true of Tijuana; and, in recent months, Tijuana as well as Mexicali has encountered all of the problems incident to a veritable population explosion.

Aerial view of San Felipe.

The Author in a curio store in San Felipe.

A hundred and twenty-five miles to the south of Mexicali is San Felipe—situated on the Gulf of California—a fishing port with an enticing Mexican atmosphere. The road is surfaced all the way, and it is possible to drive down one day, stay overnight at a good motel, explore the city, buy merchandise, and drive back across the border the next day.

We have then a Magic Square of a hundred and thirty miles containing the exotic flavor of a foreign country, enough sightseeing to satisfy the tourist as well as enough potential adventure to appeal to the explorer who wishes to get off the beaten track—all of it within a figurative stone's throw of the border.

Within this square there is an absolutely incredible assortment of fascinating country.

There are places which can be visited only with four-wheel-drive automobiles; places which can be reached only on mule back. There are cities where a person can find the charm of Old Mexico if he will but take the time to look.

Here we find a thriving, modern civilization rubbing elbows with a life so primitive that it is almost unbelievable. Here we find a country where one can enjoy all the luxuries of sophisticated foreign travel, yet within a few miles have all the adventures associated with travel in an all but unknown terrain.

It is the purpose of this book to take the reader along on some remarkably interesting exploration into this strangely contradictory Mexican square.

Another view of San Felipe.

2

Gathering of the Clan

Roscoe Hazard is a salty, whimsical, big-hearted, hard-headed fixture of San Diego. He is an expert horseman, a shrewd businessman, an adventurer, and—above all—a man who loves his friends.

Hazard has amassed a fortune in the contracting business; and so complete is his stock of ultramodern mechanized road-building equipment that it is rumored there is only one local competitor who dares to match his bids.

In recent years, "Pappy" Hazard, as he is known to his friends, has left the management of his contracting business more or less in the hands of his son Bruce, an alert, practical businessman.

It is jokingly remarked by people who know Bruce Hazard and his one principal competitor that Bruce never dares to leave San Diego until the head man of the competing firm takes a vacation. And his principal competitor, on the other hand, will never leave San Diego until he knows that Bruce will take advantage of his absence to go on a vacation. The story may be apocryphal but it is illustrative.

From a chronological standpoint, Pappy Hazard is no

Roscoe "Pappy" Hazard.

longer a young man, but in spirit he is the soul of youth.

His secretary, Nellie Miller, has been with him for years, knows his every whim, and runs her job with such smooth efficiency that Pappy Hazard never needs to bother with many of the problems which are so irritating to the average businessman. Nellie knows Pappy's friends. She knows the

Jack Trammel.

J. W. Black.

people he wants to see. She knows the people he doesn't want to see. She knows when to interrupt Pappy on one long-distance telephone call to tell him that another call is waiting.

Pappy doesn't drive a car anymore. In a hunting accident he lost the sight of one eye; so he told Bruce, "Pick out the two best drivers in the company and assign them to me."

These two men are indeed skillful drivers—and one of them, Jack Trammel, is a good camper who accompanies Pappy on most of his camping trips and who loves Pappy with a devotion equivalent to that of a loyal and affectionate son.

Pappy knew that I wanted to explore the canyons on the eastern slopes of the Sierra de Juárez. And Pappy kept pestering me on the telephone, "When are we going to start?"

It was a good question. I was for a while literally besieged with a whole series of problems. But finally I saw my way clear and gave Pappy the go-ahead sign, at the same time flashing a signal to the people who usually accompany me on my trips of exploration into Baja California.

There is J. W. Black of Paradise, California, the mechanical whiz who invented the remarkably ingenious vehicles we use in the desert and the mountains. Several years ago, when I wanted to explore the wild desert trails, I told J. W. Black what I needed. He promptly invented the Pak-Jak, which would go just about anywhere. My legs were so short and the machine so heavy that I took a couple of bad spills. So J. W. invented the Burrito—a smaller, lighter edition of the Pak-Jak.

Then I wanted something less strenuous and more stable than a two-wheeled vehicle, so J. W. obliged by inventing the Butterfly—a glorified tricycle with dual treads on all three wheels, a perfect device for searching for Indian artifacts in sandy desert soil.

But then I wanted more speed, so J. W. designed the Grasshoppper—a super dune buggy which eats up the rough desert terrain and floats over soft sand as gently as a tumbleweed.

Ricardo Castillo.

Another frequent companion is Ricardo Castillo, a young Mexican businessman—who has restaurants in Tijuana, where he serves barbecued chicken, beef, and pork cooked over the coals of ribbonwood, a relatively rare hardwood which gives a distinctive, savory flavor to whatever is cooked over the coals. Ricardo is a loyal friend, and he loves to camp. He has all the loyalties, all the instinctive courtesies, of the Mexican gentleman. If he is your friend, you are welcome to everything he has. He loves his country, its traditions, and its culture with a patriotic devotion which is both novel and refreshing in this age of general indifference to the things in life which are so truly inspirational.

Take for instance the period of recent flooding in Tijuana, when the wood trucks simply couldn't get out to bring in ordinary firewood the people needed for warmth and cooking.

Ricardo and his brother, Oswaldo, generously opened their huge reserve of rare ribbonwood which they had gathered at

Sam Hicks.

great cost. The people desperately needed wood. Each family *could* get along with just one four-foot stick which they *could* cut up into very small pieces to be used for cooking. There were a lot of families, and the expensive ribbonwood was furnished at no charge and with a smiling word of encouragement. The huge woodpile simply melted away.

The result was that when we came to Tijuana after the roads had opened, Ricardo's reserve of precious hardwood was down to virtually nothing, but the people had been able to cook their tortillas.

There is, of course, Sam Hicks, who is my right hand on any camping trip.

It simply isn't possible to describe Sam Hicks in any condensed form. Sam is a photographer, a bronc stomper, a cowboy, an outfitter, a hunter, a writer (he has recently had a book of his own, *Desert Plants and People*, published*); and

* The Naylor Company, 1966.

"Coke" Little beside his camper, chatting with J. W. Black.

Sam is one of the most skillful mountain and desert drivers I have ever known. He is six feet two of outdoor competency, and he can do anything in the out-of-doors that needs to be done.

In addition to Jack Trammel, Pappy got in touch with Elmer E. (Coke) Little, a man who has retired from active business to lead the kind of life he likes—exploring out-of-the-way country in a four-wheel-drive "camper"; a man who speaks Spanish fluently and who has his own plane. He loves to fly over difficult terrain, scouting it from a low altitude, mapping it, then picking up this four-wheel-drive camper to explore the country he has mapped—going every place that four-wheel drive can take him.

All in all, we had a remarkably efficient group. And Ricardo, who was to join us in Tecate, was bringing along a Mexican lad, Arturo Rodríguez, to assist in the camp work and generally help out all along the line.

We planned to meet at Pappy's corral early in the morning with an assortment of vehicles. In addition to our dune-buggy Grasshoppers, Pappy had his four-wheel-drive camper mounted on a G.M.C. pickup. "Coke" Little had his elaborate camper with huge retreaded airplane tires also mounted on a G.M.C. chassis. We had one camper mounted on a four-wheel-drive Ford pickup, and we had a three-quarter-ton, four-wheel-drive Ford pickup loaded with camp equipment.

We were to drive through the United States as far as Tecate, then cross over to meet Ricardo and Arturo on the Mexican side of the line.

In this way, Ricardo would not be subjected to the delay of getting crossing formalities complied with for Arturo Rodriguez.

Because we wanted an early morning start and didn't want

Starting on schedule.

to take chances on having something turn up at the last minute, Sam, J. W. Black, and I went down to San Diego late in the afternoon. Ricardo came across to join us for the evening, and we had dinner with Roscoe and Dorothea Hazard while we were making plans in detail.

We started on schedule the next morning, crossed the line at Tecate, were joined by Ricardo and Arturo; and then found that this was Flag Day in Mexico, a big holiday.

We had planned to buy fruit in Tecate—papayas, bananas, mangoes, and other perishables—but the stores were closed. Bands were parading the streets. There were speeches and a host of colorful ceremonies, with speakers addressing the huge crowd which blocked the main street.

We finally got our papers in order and moved on out of town, driving steadily until we crossed the summit of the Sierra de Juárez at an elevation of well over four thousand feet.

Holiday in Tecate.

Band lining up to parade.

Over the divide, we found a wide place in the road where we could park our caravan and have lunch—looking down the sheer slopes of the mountain to the shimmering desert below.

We got out the lunch, and it turned out to be quite a lunch.

It was then we started to compare notes.

Roscoe Hazard had insisted that he wanted to buy some of the provisions. Sam had pointed out that on a trip of this sort it is better for one person to plan the meals and pick up the groceries. But Pappy finally said, "Well, let me pick up the meat."

So Sam agreed to let him pick up the meat.

Then Pappy had pointed out that he liked lots of salads when he camped. He felt that the Tijuana fruit and vegetable market had better romaine lettuce than any other place within a hundred miles. So Ricardo had agreed to buy the romaine lettuce real early in the morning so it would be fresh.

Lunch in a wide place on the road.

Fruit and vegetable market in Tijuana. Ricardo Castillo and Sam Hicks on the extreme right.

Ricardo bought a crate of romaine lettuce.

(The Tijuana market is open long before the ones on the United States side of the border.)

While we were having lunch we took inventory of what we had, and it turned out that Pappy Hazard had purchased a hundred and sixty-two dollars' worth of steaks alone—to say nothing of roasts, ground round, bacon, and chops.

The Hazard camper was quite a deal, and so was the camper of Coke Little. These outfits had refrigerators which could get meat so cold it was frozen stiff, and in addition to this we had well-insulated camping iceboxes.

We then discovered that Ricardo had purchased a full case of crisp, garden-fresh romaine lettuce—and did it come in handy out there in the desert!

Ricardo had a way of trimming off all of the leaves except the choice, crisp center parts. Sam had a formula for salad dressing which he insisted was "an old family secret"; and that lettuce, coming cool and crisp off the ice, made salads which were heaven-sent delicacies in the hot reaches of the Laguna Salada.

Arturo Rodríguez washing breakfast dishes with water from the hot springs in Guadalupe Canyon.

We finished lunch and descended the long winding grade, which is a wonderful piece of mountain road engineering, and so came at length to the desert. Then we turned from the highway and started slogging along on dirt roads, some of which were surprisingly good considering the terrain.

Late in the afternoon we turned to the west and started up the fairly well-known canyon which leads to Guadalupe. And shortly before dark we came to a gate where a rancher charges two dollars a car for camping privileges on a beautiful palm-covered plateau a relatively short distance up the canyon.

The approach to this plateau, however, is on a road so steep that it takes a pickup or a four-wheel-drive automobile to make it.

We went through the gate, up the grade, and came to a scene of indescribable beauty. A stream of water was running right through the camp. There was level ground shaded by palm trees. In addition, there was a hot mineral spring which had been covered over with a thatched hut so as to make a beautiful bathtub. It had a goodly current of hot water flowing through it, giving the bather a gentle water massage.

We spread out our camping equipment, made camp, got a fire going; and when the fire got down to coals, we unwrapped some of Hazard's packages of meat.

Those were real steaks.

Hazard had impressed upon his favorite butcher the fact that he wanted steaks that would melt in your mouth, and he wanted them cut *thick*.

There were steaks and steaks and steaks, and they were cut thick. And Sam started barbecuing them over the coals.

Soon our rancher host showed up with his children, who gathered around the campfire, unmistakably expecting an invitation to dinner—an invitation which was gladly extended.

That was a deluxe camp.

When I camp I like to have chairs—lots of chairs. We carry folding aluminum chairs and chaise longues. They don't weigh much and, when they are folded, they don't take up too much room. We always carry enough chairs so that we have plenty for ourselves and for any guests who may drop in.

We also carry ice-cold beer and soda pop of different flavors. We had managed to find a liquor store open at Tecate and we had laid in a supply of Bacardi rum, whisky, gin, vodka, and tequila.

So we sat around the campfire having appetizers, watching Sam cook the steaks to broiled perfection while we sipped various cocktails—my own preference in Mexico being chilled, canned grapefruit juice laced with Bacardi rum.

We parked among the palm trees at the hot springs in Guadalupe
Canyon.

That was a real repast. Sourdough French bread toasted
and mellowed with melted butter. Beans and tortillas which
Ricardo had brought from his restaurant in Tijuana. Steak
and crisp salad, and ice-cold canned peaches for dessert.

Roscoe Hazard is quite a camper, and he has discovered
certain things which go fine on a camping trip. One of his
favorites is a particular brand of canned peach halves in
heavy syrup, kept on ice.

We were good and sleepy shortly after we finished eating,
and we rolled in.

Sometime during the night I was awakened by the sound of
an exhaust. Then more exhausts. Then cars, then voices, then
more cars and more voices.

It turned out that an entire four-wheel-drive club of heaven
knows how many vehicles had decided to make the run from
their home town to Guadalupe Canyon.

They evidently expected to find the place deserted so they
could take it over. And when they arrived late at night, tired
and hungry, and found the choice camping spots preempted,

they drove around and around in the night searching with flashlights, trying to find the next best places.

However, I was too blissfully happy to worry much about it and went back to sleep in the middle of all the noise.

I was sleeping in the camper, and getting back to sleep was easy. The others, who had their sleeping bags out in the open, found it rather annoying to have cars driving by, lights playing over the beds, and voices in their ears.

It was just one of those things which wouldn't happen very often, but it happened.

When we got up in the morning we decided that we were going to move. The place was simply crawling with people; and, since they were people who knew each other well and had been on many trips together, we felt something like interlopers—despite the fact we had been there first.

However, we had heard so much about Guadalupe Canyon, and the scenery which was to be found above camp after a mile and a half hike on a trail, that we decided Sam would take a quick trip up this trail with Coke Little to see for himself just what the scenery was like—and get some photographs.

If the scenery warranted, we intended to return to Guadalupe Canyon at a later date, when it was not so crowded. And since this was a weekend and since the canyon is fairly well known to four-wheel-drive clubs, we realized it would be better to return sometime during the middle of the following week.

While Sam and Coke Little were up the canyon, the others got the camp loaded in the automobiles; and by the time Sam was back with an enthusiastic account of the scenery, the camp was ready to roll.

After hearing Sam's description, we all decided that we would return to the Guadalupe camp during the middle of the week.

"Coke" Little above the waterfall and deep pool at the head of Guadalupe Canyon.

Guadalupe Canyon is a beautiful place. The palm-lined floor stretches far back into the Sierra de Juárez. There is a stream running down the canyon, hot sulphur springs are on the mesa, and at the end of the trail up the canyon is a beautiful waterfall where the stream makes a sheer drop into a deep pool of crystal-clear water.

The canyon derives its name from a peculiar rock pinnacle at the skyline of the high mountains. This pinnacle seems to be the statue of the Virgin casting a benediction over the country below and towering majestically, bathed in gold with the rays of the morning sun.

When we had our camp loaded we returned to the main road down the Laguna Salada.

Pappy Hazard finds a horse to ride in the well-watered Palomar Canyon.

More and more I was impressed with the beauty and the magnitude of this country, but also with its potential dangers. Here is a section of wicked, treacherous desert which can be a veritable furnace in the summer. Even as it was, in the dead of winter we could feel the power of the desert sun.

Coke Little had flown over this section of desert repeatedly, and when he knew we were planning this trip he had made several low-level flights in his airplane to check on landmarks and make an accurate map of the country.

Moreover, Little knew the rancher who controlled a well-watered canyon some thirty or forty miles to the south in an air line, a canyon named Palomar in which there were reputed to be between twenty and thirty thousand palm trees and where

Three woodchoppers saved from a seventy-five-mile walk by our Grasshoppers.

Pappy, who likes to do his exploring on horseback, could find a horse to ride. It was in completely primitive country with many *borrego,* or mountain sheep, in the surrounding hills.

As we progressed during the day, the hot sun begun to beat down upon us—despite the fact that it was still early in February and for the most part the United States was covered with a blanket of snow and ice, with blizzards sweeping through the Midwest. Our radios told us of stalled traffic and snow-choked streets in New York and Chicago. All around us the desert blazed in sunlight.

As we pushed on, the road gradually began to deteriorate and became a little harder to follow. Here and there were branch roads taking off and leading somewhere or other, but since Coke had charted the country by airplane he was able to keep us going in the right direction.

At length we came to a road leading to a ranch where Coke wanted to stop long enough to say hello; and we followed this road back into the mouth of the canyon, finding a rancher who had dug a well, had struck large quantities of water, and was irrigating an alfalfa field. He also had quite a cattle ranch in operation.

We visited at this ranch for a while and then went back to the main road, following it on down to a place where there had been a corral and a well. Then we turned and started up toward the mountains.

Abruptly we came on three men walking as rapidly as they could through the afternoon heat—and were they glad to see us!

We gave them water, which they drank eagerly from one of our canteens, and learned that they were woodcutters whose truck had broken down. They were faced with the necessity of walking to Mexicali—some seventy-five miles across the burning desert. They said they hoped to catch a ride if they got to the main wood-chopping road in time to make contact with one of the woodcutters.

This wood and wood-chopping is an interesting phase of Mexican life.

In Mexican cities much of the cooking is done with wood; and since the cities have been there for many, many years, the wood has been gradually depleted until it is no longer possible for the householder to go out and pick up a few limbs to make a fire on which to warm up his tortillas.

Therefore there are woodcutters who take burros and go out into the canyons, cutting the choice hardwoods such as mesquite and ironwood, loading their burros with these sticks of wood, and then going back the long distance to town.

In Tijuana and Mexicali, which have a more sophisticated environment and where the closer supplies of wood are largely depleted, the wood gathering is done by using trucks.

These woodcutters' trucks usually have a complement of three men. They go far out into the canyons, traveling perhaps for a day. Then they cut and load wood for one or two days. Then they take the load back to the city.

These woodcutters get from forty to fifty dollars for a truckload of wood. They have to pay two assistants. They have to pay for gasoline. They have to pay for tires and maintenance of the truck. Yet they manage somehow to make a living by dint of hard work.

In a country where there are no shortcuts to wealth, where the economy is tight, the things that have to be done are done.

Since the men were in a hurry to cover the weary miles to the main woodchoppers' road, and since we quite apparently were a bunch of United States tourists, it was evident they had little expectation of any help other than the drinking water and the food which we gave them.

When we inquired in detail as to their plight and found that they would have to walk some fifteen miles before dark, and then might have to walk another thirty or forty miles to the main highway, we told them to climb aboard two of the Grasshoppers; we said we'd take them down to the woodchoppers' road so that they could get a ride back to Mexicali on one of the trucks.

To say that they were agreeably surprised is very, very much of an understatement.

These Grasshoppers are made from shortened Volkswagen chassis. Their high-flotation soft-pressure tires and individual wheel suspension makes them able to float over the desert at high speed, going over rough roads that a truck or an ordinary four-wheel-drive automobile must take slowly—and even then with spine-pounding jars which can become very wearying. The Grasshoppers ride unbelievably smoothly and fairly eat up the desert miles.

J. W. Black and Ricardo felt that they could take two Grasshoppers and not only take these woodcutters back to the road where some other woodcutting truck would pick them up that night, but that they could make the round trip in time to join us at the place where we would be turning off in order to go up Palomar Canyon.

So the woodcutters climbed aboard the Grasshoppers. We started our caravan in motion again and continued on through the afternoon, coming at length to the place where we turned off and where we were to wait for the Grasshoppers.

We didn't have long to wait. Within less than half an hour, which we put in taking photographs and stretching our legs, the Grasshoppers were back with the report that the wood-cutters had enjoyed the ride so much that they hated to see their destination come in sight.

The road turned off here, and we skirted a hill and crossed a barranca to come to a country where the desert was more productive of vegetation.

Soon we began to get into mesquite trees, ironwood trees, and evidences of the activities of woodchoppers. Then we came to the broken-down truck which had been abandoned by our three friends when the transmission went out. It was sitting squarely in the middle of the road, loaded with wood, and we had to go into four-wheel-drive to get around it. Getting this truck out of there would be a real problem for the alert-looking young Mexican businessman who had been the head of the expedition.

We moved onward through the afternoon, the road becoming more and more rough; in places it was literally covered with rocks, from a foot to two feet in diameter, which slowed our progress to a crawl.

We worked up a sandy wash, then climbed above it to a side hill, and after a while began to see palm trees. Then we moved along through a desert which was becoming ever more covered with various trees—the verde tree, the smoke tree, the giant cacti, ironwood, and mesquite.

The woodchoppers' broken-down truck.

Quite late in the afternoon we came to a steep grade down into a dry stream bed and encountered a fence and a gate.

We went through this gate, drove for half or three-quarters of a mile, and came to the little cattle ranch of Señor Antonio Dowling.

Coke Little was acquainted with Señor Dowling, and we readily received permission to camp and were welcomed with the open hospitality of the Mexican rancher.

The ranch shelter at the moment consisted of a small thatched hut. The ranch house had recently caught fire and burned down.

Señor Dowling and four or five vaqueros were living here under exceedingly primitive conditions, and yet they had everything they really wanted.

There was a beautiful stream of clear, sweet water running

Slowed to a crawl.

The ranch shelter consisted of a small thatched hut.

An army of palms.

down the canyon. Farther up the canyon there was a hot spring and a natural bathing pool; and everywhere were palms, palms by the hundreds, palms casting a deep shade and furnishing shelter for thousands of quail and doves.

The long, lazy cooing of the white-winged dove was constantly in our ears. The quail were so plentiful they could have been shot with a .22 revolver if one had been minded to get a mess of them.

However, we still had Pappy's hundred and sixty-two dollars' worth of steaks, to say nothing of the roasts and the huge blocks of frozen ground round steak.

Señor Dowling listened to one of us stating that Pappy had spent a hundred and sixty-two dollars for steaks and said lugubriously, "Why didn't you come here? I would have sold you a whole steer for twenty dollars, and butchered it to boot."

Señor Dowling.

Here was a beautiful camp. We had none of the distractions we had had the night before. We had the canyon all to ourselves except for the vaqueros who, now that we were guests of the ranch, accepted us without question, coming in to join us for dinner.

Once more we had barbecued steaks and some of that wonderful crisp salad made of the choice parts of the lettuce leaves.

We had tortillas, beans, canned vegetables, and again cold canned peaches for dessert.

Then we sat around the campfire saying but little, yet having that warm feeling of friendship which comes so easily in Mexico.

Suddenly a coyote barked, startlingly close to camp. There was a moment's silence. Then another coyote barked.

When we had a tame coyote living in the hills at our ranch

Many coyotes live here.

I had learned the trick of pitching my voice into a shrill falsetto and giving two or three quick barks; these evidently meant something in coyote talk, because our coyote would always answer me.

This time I barked and was surprised to find that I was answered by what must have been a dozen coyotes, all apparently within two or three hundred yards of camp. The place was literally crawling with coyotes.

A camp of this sort represents an element of danger because occasionally there is a rabid coyote. It is for that reason that I like to carry a .22 revolver when I am in Mexico—or, as far as that is concerned, when I am camping in the desert regions of California.

David Hurtado, who works for us, had an experience with a rabid coyote. He had stopped the pickup he was driving, to open a gate, when the coyote came charging at him. David had enough presence of mind to jump back into the car and slam the door shut. The coyote hurled himself at the glass window, slobbering and panting, biting frantically, trying to get at David inside the car.

David had to turn the car and make a long run, with the coyote chasing him; then he turned completely around and dashed back at full speed in order to have a chance to get out of the car, and open and close the gate, before the coyote— who by this time was pretty much exhausted—came into sight.

One wonders how rabies is ever controlled.

An infected coyote must bite several other coyotes during the course of his illness, and those coyotes, in turn, must bite others. Yet somehow the disease seems eventually to control itself, and it is only occasionally one encounters a rabid coyote or the results of a rabid coyote's bite.

It is not generally known, but steers on the range can get rabies from the bite of an infected coyote. And, of course, it is well known that bats can become infected with hydrophobia and represent a dangerous source of infection to humans.

Once, years ago, I encountered a rabid skunk. And twice I have found bats lying on the ground under such circumstances that I promptly dispatched them and got them out of the way because I thought they were suffering from rabies. But to my knowledge I have never seen a rabid coyote.

With all of the camping I have done, sleeping for the most part on the ground out in the open, in country that is heavily populated with coyotes, we have never had the slightest trouble.

One night, however, down in Baja California when I was in my sleeping bag, dead to the world, I became drowsily aware that some heavy-furred animal had crawled up on my stomach and was lying there with his warm fur directly under my chin.

I tried to get awake enough to reach for a flashlight and

Thatched shelter near our camp in Palomar Canyon.

find out what it was all about, but the sleeping bag was warm, the night outside was cold, and I was sleepy. I gave the problem drowsy consideration, and the first thing I knew I had gone to sleep again. I struggled awake and the animal was still there. Then I sank into deep slumber, and by morning my visitor was gone.

It may have been some dog that had crawled in looking for warmth, but there were no ranches nearby. I don't know. I never will know.

According to plans, we were to stay at the Palomar Canyon camp for a day and a half, and then return to Guadalupe during the middle of the week—when we could expect to find that we had the beautiful little plateau all to ourselves.

However, this camping in the Palomar Canyon was so absolutely, wonderfully ideal that we hesitated to tear ourselves away. And then it turned out that I of all people, veteran camper that I am, had gone along on the trip with all of my cameras but had left all of my surplus film at home; we had only the film in the cameras.

Sam, J. W., Coke, and Ricardo rose to the occasion. They would take the Grasshoppers and make a quick run into Mexicali and back, picking up some film in Calexico.

Of course, we strongly suspected that what they really wanted was an adventurous ride in the Grasshoppers. And it certainly is fun—when you are unhampered by keeping in a procession with heavily laden pickups—to take these cute little bugs and go skimming over the desert roads at forty or fifty miles an hour in place of the sedate fifteen miles per hour that is the usual speed of the caravan.

In any event, we decided that this was the thing to do; and so we settled down into a luxurious camp, drenched in a warm sunlight which up there in the canyon was near the ideal temperature. Even if it got a little too warm in the direct rays of the sun, it was just right to sit in shirt sleeves in the shade of the palm trees.

We sat there listening to the cooing of the doves, talking, taking pictures from time to time, and just relaxing.

Inevitably, however, Jack Trammel began to get a little restless and hinted that Pappy was a great poker player.

After he had told me for about the fifth time how much Pappy liked to play poker and how good he was at it, I yielded and said, "All right, Jack. Get the cards."

Now, I had heard a lot about Pappy's poker playing. People who had stood on the sidelines and watched games in which Pappy Hazard had been a player spoke with bated breath of his prowess. It seems some of those games were big, with several thousand dollars in the pot in the middle of the table.

I love to play poker, but I am not a gambler. I don't want to play in a game where I can get hurt and I don't want to play in a game where anybody else can get hurt. And lots of times I play games where people who are working for me, and who might be inclined to plunge, are sitting in the game.

Therefore I have adopted a rule that in all of our games in camp there is a one-cent ante and a two-bit limit, with a limit on the number of raises that can be made on any one hand.

I think in all of our poker games the most that has ever been won or lost by anyone is something under five dollars.

When I communicated these rules to Pappy Hazard he looked at me in open-mouthed astonishment and then consternation.

"What's the matter?" he asked. "Don't you make enough money out of writing your books to play poker?"

I looked him right in the eye and said, "No."

Pappy heaved a sigh. He is an inveterate poker player, and he would rather play poker for a penny ante than not play poker at all.

So Pappy, Jack, and I got in Pappy's camper and brought out the poker chips.

From time to time Pappy shook his head. "I've heard about your blankety-blank version of this game," he said at length in a tone of exasperation, "but so help me God I never thought I'd be playing it."

Pappy is quite a poker player. His first job is to upset the other players so that they don't know whether they're coming or going. You deal Pappy a hand. He'll take a look at his hand with a typical poker face. Somebody opens for a nickel.

"Up two bits," says Pappy without hesitation.

A couple of fainthearted players will drop out. The man who opens the pot will reluctantly see the raise. He probably opened on a fairly low pair and hoped to better them on the draw.

Pappy, who has boosted the bet to the limit, will promptly

Pappy picks up his hand, doesn't like the cards . . .

. . . then decides to bluff.

PaiPai Indians.

throw four cards into the discard and say, "Give me four cards."

However, the guy's luck is such that on that four-card draw to an ace he's just as apt as not to catch two more aces. He is a deadly, dangerous, poker player, and he's dangerous because you can't figure out his game.

After his four-card draw Pappy is again apt to raise any bet that is made. At the end of the betting he may have three aces, or he may have nothing.

He is, in short, one of those fellows who can keep the other players off balance.

When a game has a two-bit limit it's pretty difficult to upset other players in this manner. But if, instead of tossing two bits into the pot, a player can say, "Fifty dollars," and then, "Up another hundred," the situation can become very disturbing to a man who is trying to play good conservative poker. Personally, I like to play poker where the conversation over the

poker table is the main ingredient and the money only a sec-
ondary consideration.

Pappy wrestled with that penny-ante poker playing for a
while and then he looked at me beseechingly.

"Erle, will you do me a favor?"

"What?" I asked.

"Please," he said, "please, will you let me make the ante two
cents?"

I leaned toward him so that there would be no chance for a
misunderstanding and shouted, "*No!*"

Pappy was licked. He settled back and resigned himself to
playing penny ante.

That night the folks got back from Mexicali long after dark,
and we had been really worried about them. It turned out
they had decided to go to Mexicali the long way around,
skirting Laguna Salada, going down through the mountains,
then on down to the river at El Mayor, then going into
Mexicali.

They had had a wonderful trip and returned in high spirits,
enthused over their discovery of a pass through the mountains
along a faint road which Coke Little had spotted from the air.

We started laying plans, and it was unanimously decided
that we would pass up returning to Guadalupe; instead, we
would press on south and try to get to the land of the PaiPai
Indians and back, taking only one pickup and the two Grasshoppers. And so that we could make better time, we kept the
pickup loaded with just enough ballast to make it ride easy.

That next day we had a marvelous time. We went back to
the edge of Laguna Salada and then went on south, mile after
mile over the desert, until finally we came to a landmark
which Little had spotted from the air; here we turned up a
canyon, eventually coming to a little village of the PaiPai
Indians.

These Indians are a remarkably interesting group and ap-

Juan Arballo.

parently exceedingly healthy. One of the senior citizens of the place, Juan Arballo, had an impressive attitude of great dignity. He seemed to be a leader of the tribe and at first was a bit standoffish. But when it appeared he had worked for Coke Little's father many years before, he became very cordial.

We didn't realize it at the time, but we were destined to see a great deal more of Juan Arballo as we explored Mexico's Magic Square.

It is reported that the PaiPai country is simply crawling with deer, which is probably true.

When residents kill deer only for food there is usually an abundance of deer. Paradoxically enough, it is the closing of hunting season which exterminates deer.

This, of course, needs a little explaining.

When the season is closed, the deer are protected against everyone except poachers. But when you have a closed season on deer, the corollary is that at some time during the late summer or early fall the season must open.

What happens when you have an opening of a season that has been closed for several months?

The sporting-goods stores put up window displays featuring synthetic campfires of red crepe paper actuated by an electric fan with red electric bulbs underneath, with dummy figures sitting around surrounded by all sorts of camping paraphernalia.

The opening of deer season is Big Business.

The sporting-goods stores sell ammunition, rifles, sleeping bags, tents, red hats, hiking boots, snakebite remedies, hunting knives, compasses, waterproof match cases, gasoline stoves, and all of the other gear which goes with camping and hunting.

Cash registers jingle a merry tune.

The day before the opening of deer season dawns. Hunters from all over the country pour into the foothills, start climbing the mountain roads. Little restaurants are jammed to capacity. Gasoline stations are selling gas just as fast as the pumps will work. Grocery stores and markets in the deer country are doing a land-office business.

Hunters move on into camp. Campfires dot the mountains like luminous pinpoints.

Comes the dawn.

Bang . . . Powie . . . Powie, powie, powie . . . Bang . . . Bang

. . . Powie, bang, powie, bang, powie.

Hunters are hiding behind every bush. The confused deer, running from one hunter, dash headlong into another hunter, then turn in panic only to find themselves in a cross fire from still another two hunters.

A sporting-goods store offers a cash prize for the first person to check in a legal deer. A newspaper offers a prize for the biggest deer.

For one nightmarish day the deer have no place to go, no place to hide. Confused, bewildered, many of them wounded, they seek places of concealment.

Deer by the hundreds are brought out through the game-checking stations, transported to town, skinned, cut up, and placed in refrigerators.

This is what comes of protecting deer by a closed season. A closed season means a big day of opening season. A big day of opening season means literally hundreds of dead and wounded deer.

There are many parts of Mexico where wild game is the only fresh meat obtainable except, perhaps, when some rancher has a herd of goats. Yet in those parts of Mexico where the sportsmen-hunters have left the game alone, it is usually relatively easy for a native to go out and bag a deer, quite frequently with nothing more formidable in the way of a weapon than a .22-caliber gun.

Quail are quite frequently snared and used for food regardless of season, and yet the birds seem plentiful.

This, of course, isn't true in the cities, but it is true in the isolated ranchos out in the country, and particularly in the little Indian settlements.

I didn't ask specifically in the village of the PaiPai Indians; but I saw deer tracks, and I have a feeling that these Indians either live off the country or supplement their diet with what

J. W. Black inspects "jerky" being dried.

the country has to offer. I know that some of them take game with bow and arrow.

The Mexicans have for years had to get along without refrigeration of any sort. Therefore, when they kill meat, they dry it in the sun, making a species of "Jerky" which is dry and hard—and which will, of course, keep almost indefinitely.

Then they take out a piece of this hard dried meat, put it on a hard board, and pound it into powder. This powdered dried meat is mixed with onions, garlic, chili sauce and herbs, and makes a dish which is hard on tender teeth but which certainly sticks to one's ribs.

We visited with the PaiPai Indians and found them so cordial and interesting that it was hard to get away; and yet we knew that time was rapidly running out if we were to get back to camp.

In books on Mexico written half a century ago, the land of the PaiPais was virtually unknown, and the few travelers who

The Author making friends with the dogs of the PaiPai Indians.

did know of it shunned the area and tried never to spend a night there.

This was, of course, a long, long time ago. Now we found the Indians clean, friendly, well nourished, good natured and hospitable.

They had water for irrigation. They had fields which were planted and well tended and they seemed happy and prosperous although probably the net annual income of any individual measured in terms of money would have been microscopic as compared with our standards.

I certainly enjoyed the dogs. They wanted to protect the Indians and bristled at our approach. But after being assured that we were all right, they subsided; and later on, when I moved around taking pictures and would go into the backyard or unexpectedly come around the corner of a building, one of these dogs would at first bare his teeth; then, recognizing me as one who had previously been cleared, he

A PaiPai Indian dog sleeping in the sun.

would lower his lips. And at the end of our visit he would even dubiously wag his tail in a half-hearted way, showing a limited recognition of the hospitality which had been extended to us by the Indians.

I think these people like to consider themselves a distinct ethnic group. When one of the dogs first bared his teeth at us, I said something to the effect that he was a good Mexican watchdog and wasn't going to let any gringos come into camp. One of the Indians who was standing nearby promptly corrected me by saying that he was a good PaiPai dog.

These dogs were well fed, well mannered, and, I think, efficient watchdogs, keeping coyotes away from the places which house the chickens at night—although these houses were so constructed that it would have taken a coyote with a can opener and a crowbar to get into them.

Reluctantly we said our farewells and departed for camp, arriving late in the afternoon, in time to have one of Pappy's

big roasts cooked in a Dutch oven. And again we had the
vaqueros with us for company.

This was to be our last evening in camp, so I asked Ricardo
to interpret for me and told Señor Dowling how much we
appreciated his hospitality. I said I was not in a position to
make him a gift at the moment because we had been so heavily loaded and because I hadn't had a chance to buy any gifts
before I left; I would, however, appreciate it as a personal
favor if he would let me leave some cash with him, and at
some suitable time when he found himself in Mexicali he
could purchase some article as a gift from me.

The man straightened in his chair and said that he didn't
accept pay for his hospitality, that we were welcome.

I then had some difficulty in having Ricardo explain to him
again that we were not trying to pay him for his hospitality,
that I was only asking him to cooperate with me in getting
himself a gift.

At that the man began to smile. His manner softened and
he said, "Upon that basis I will gladly accept the money."

I think it is always a good idea to try to leave some money
with people who own ranches and extend camping privileges.
In many instances they expect it. In many instances they do
not. But I feel it should always be tendered with just the right
attitude and in just the right manner.

The same is true of visiting with any of the Indian tribes. I
think it is advisable to give presents wherever possible, and
I do not think it is advisable to try to pay people for the privilege of taking their pictures.

If people don't want their pictures taken, that's all there is
to it. Make no attempt to click the shutter. If, however, people are willing to pose for pictures, it is then always permissi-
ble when parting company to give them either some present
in the form of merchandise or some little donation of cash.
But everything depends upon the manner in which this is

The bullring in Tijuana.

The Author showered with gifts by Tijuana's welcoming committee.

Pappy Hazard and Jack Trammel in camp.

The Author.

The Blimp takes off for Mexico.

Coke Little drinks from stream in country purported to be all desert.

En route to Mexico.

The weather took a turn for the worse.

Our host, Señor Dowling, rides into camp.

done. And, above all, one should avoid being patronizing or in any way condescending.

To point a camera at a stranger is presumptive. Later on, after you have shown an interest in him and have become friends, is the time to bring up tactfully the subject of pictures.

3

A Quick Look at Mexicali

One of the objectives of our trip was to visit the CETYS University at Mexicali.

I had been hearing a lot about this. Roscoe Hazard has been one of the sponsors. And my friend Lic. Ignacio Guajardo is President of the Instituto Educativo del Noroeste.

Lic. Ignacio Guajardo is a very remarkable individual, a patriotic Mexican, a bilingual attorney (the abbreviation Lic. stands for Licenciado, which is the official Mexican designation for an attorney who has been licensed to practice law in Mexico). I have known him for about twenty years, and he and Pappy are fast friends.

When I told Licenciado Guajardo that we were going to take a camera and explore some of the area of northern Baja California, he at once suggested that we visit the university.

So after we broke camp at the Palomar we drove into Mexicali, then crossed the line to Calexico; there my executive secretary Jean Bethell, who has been with me for so many years, joined the expedition, carrying a suitcase full of clean clothes for me—which came in very handy indeed.

The only fly in the ointment was that my close friend,

Pappy Hazard, left, with our friend, Lic. Ignacio Guajardo.

Colonel José Gutiérrez, was not home but was atttending to business in Mexico City. However, I promised that I would get back at a later date to see him and at that time get a little more information on Baja California.

Colonel Gutiérrez has from time to time accompanied me on my expeditions into Baja California. We have spent many an hour together, sitting around a campfire or adventuring in automobiles or airplanes.

He is one of the prominent public-spirited citizens of Mexicali, has a big ranch to the south of the city, and he has, from time to time, tried his hand at various commercial enterprises in order to furnish employment to as many people as possible.

His house is a beautiful and comfortable home with lots of elbow room; and his wife, Emily, is a marvelous hostess.

We have known Joe and Emily for many, many years. They are warm, loyal friends and have frequently visited at my ranch at Temecula.

The spacious home of Colonel Gutiérrez, in Mexicali.

Colonel Gutiérrez is an accomplished flier with a long military history. He was an ace during Mexico's revolution, when using airplanes in combat was very much of a novelty. He is an expert horseman and is, I believe, responsible for the founding of the Mexicali Riding Club, although Licenciado Guajardo also joined in the organization of the club; and both men have been enthusiastic supporters ever since its beginnings.

This Mexicali Riding Club is a wonderful asset to the social life of Mexicali, is fine training for the young ladies and young gentlemen who are growing up in the community, and is a means of enjoyment for their fathers.

Colonel Gutiérrez loves to train horses to jump, and both he and Licenciado Guajardo enjoy riding jumping horses. They work up from the low jumps to the real high ones, until finally they are riding dangerously, sitting on a horse that is clearing every inch he can possibly clear.

Guajardo's daughters, Griselda and Alida.

Left to right: Alejandro, Juan Ignacio, Alida, and Griselda Guajardo on their splendid horses.

Major Juan Flores Pérez.

For some years the club has employed Major Juan Flores Pérez as its trainer and as its on-the-ground manager.

Major Flores is a lean ex-cavalryman who loves horses, likes to train them, knows just about all there is to know about jumping horses; and he is in superb physical condition despite the fact he is no longer a young man.

So our crowd went to El Rancho Motel in Calexico, enjoyed the luxury of a hot bath with lots of soap and an abundance of hot water, put on clean clothes, and sallied forth with various remarks to each other as to what had happened to the smell and "how nice you look without the whiskers."

Licenciado Guajardo escorted us to the university.

I wish it were possible to describe some things in words and to describe them adequately.

If a man had to describe the color yellow or the odor of violets without having anything to use as a standard of comparison it would be an impossible assignment. And the experience we had at the university is equally difficult to describe.

The faculty were there to meet us, but before we entered the place I had to stop to admire the architecture.

There is something about Mexican architecture that simply fascinates me. The architects have a virile ability to break away from tradition, to design a building which suits the mood and the purpose of its existence, and to give the entire structure a dynamic symmetry which challenges the attention. Mexican architecture reaches heights of creative achievement that are at times breathtaking.

Major Pérez taking the high jump.

Lic. Carlos Padilla Ibarra and Dr. Felix Castillo Jiménez greet the Author.

Roscoe E. Hazard, Lic. Ignacio Guajardo, and the Author in front of CETYS University.

This university building had been constructed on pillars to provide a gathering place in the shade underneath. The outer walls were latticed for ventilation and view, yet the openings were small enough to prevent drafts.

The over-all outline, the sweep of the staircases, the manner in which the supporting pillars had been placed, gave the total concept a strength, a vigor, a feeling of youth seeking the answer to the problems of the world.

We stood for several minutes looking at that building, admiring the structure as a whole and the way it was laid out. Then we moved forward to find a welcoming committee ready to receive us.

I think we were all tremendously impressed with the cali-

Sr. Miguel Angel Moreno Cota, a newspaper reporter, the Author, Lic. Carlos Padilla Ibarra, Dr. Felix Castillo Jiménez, and Lic. Ignacio Guajardo.

ber of the faculty and the appearance of the students.

The professors who met us were alert, wide-awake individuals who had a tremendous enthusiasm for their calling.

The students we encountered were earnest young people who were attending the college for the purpose of getting an education.

We entered the classrooms, and the material on the blackboards showed that the courses were geared for good hard work.

I understand there is a similar university in Monterrey, Mexico, and that these are the only two privately supported universities in northern Mexico.

More power to them.

We had a most enjoyable visit, and while I was there I was forced to think of the public spirit of the men who accompanied us: Ignacio Guajardo, who has devoted much of his time and energy to promoting CETYS; and Roscoe Hazard, who has not only given much of his valuable time to the university but who has also financially aided an occassional student.

These activities are very much worth while. A man can have a sense of deep satisfaction in knowing that he is helping one of the younger generation to cope with an environment which is becoming increasingly complex. I don't suppose the professors at this university are ever going to get rich, certainly not on a professor's salary, but I have seldom seen people so enthusiastic about the work they have chosen for their careers.

The Author with a group of students.

4

Blimping over Baja

My explorations of Baja California have been by jeep, by airplane, by helicopter, by Grasshopper, by Butterfly, and by Pak-Jak.

Yet I wanted a new approach.

The whole thing started when Sam Hicks and I were making a rush trip to Tijuana to confer with Ricardo Castillo over how to get pictures which would tell the story of Tijuana.

The story of Tijuana is difficult to get and more difficult to write. This is probably because there are three Tijuanas. First, there is the Tijuana that the tourist sees. Second, there is the Tijuana that is related to the bullfights, the dog races, and the horse races. The people who attend these usually care little about the rest of the city. Third, there is the part of Tijuana the tourist never sees, the side of the city composed of professional men, of businessmen, the high-ranking officials, the attorneys, the doctors, the judges.

And the story of Tijuana as it is seen by the tourist is also divided into layers. There are tourists who are looking for vice. There are tourists who are looking for curios. There are tourists who simply want to send souvenir postal cards to

70

Our fleet of campers, four-wheel-drive trucks, Grasshoppers, and . . .

. . . the Butterfly.

their friends. These tourists want to be able to state that they have been in Mexico; and since Tijuana is only a few miles from San Diego, they decide to make a round trip and stay long enough to pick up some little souvenir.

Suffice it to say it is the most popular tourist city in the world, outranking Rome, Paris, London, Buenos Aires. The aggregate number of tourists who go to Tijuana is simply staggering. Nearly a million and a half tourists go to Tijuana every month, some fifty-five thousand a day. It seems incredible, but it is a fact.

Yet far too many of the tourists drive aimlessly around town, search perhaps in vain for a parking space, stay for from forty-five minutes to an hour and a half, and then return to the United States.

Tijuana has suffered because of a poor image—a reputation for honky-tonks, stripteases, and prostitution.

Far too few people have ever explored the attractive parts of Tijuana which appeal so strongly to the tourist who is fortunate enough to find them.

There are furniture factories in Tijuana where beautiful furniture is made from imported woods. There are leather factories where all sorts of fine hand-tooled leather can be obtained at moderate prices. There is a factory where plaques and inlays are made with an artistry and grace which is inconceivable. There are all sorts of high-class stores, and some of the finest food in the world at some of the best restaurants.

The big trouble with Tijuana is that it just grew without any planning, without any zoning, and it is such a thriving metropolis that the casual tourist can very quickly become confused.

I wanted to tell the world something about the real Tijuana; but in dealing with a problem of this magnitude, where is one going to begin? How is one going to get an angle that will hold the attention of the reader and, at the same time, tell the story?

While Sam and I were driving along and talking it over, I looked up into the sky and saw the Goodyear blimp.

That Goodyear blimp is a familiar sight, particularly on the West Coast of the United States (I understand there is another one on the East Coast which is, I believe, based in Miami).

I had always taken it for granted that the blimp was simply used as a portable billboard in the sky, a huge dirigible with the name "Goodyear" painted on it in letters so large they could be read for miles. And of course I knew that from time to time the blimp was used for a public service, such as hovering over the famous Tournament of Roses Festival in Pasadena on New Year's Day.

An idea struck me. Why not get the Goodyear dirigible to perform another public service by helping to tell the story of Tijuana, Ensenada, and Mexicali?

After all, the Goodyear Tire and Rubber Company was engaged in global business. It was keenly conscious of international problems not only in commerce but also in friendship. What better gesture could be made to the people of Baja California than to send the blimp down on a goodwill tour, attracting attention to the border cities, conveying a message of brotherhood and, incidentally, giving us a platform from which we could take much better pictures of Baja California than would be possible from a swift-flying airplane (with its attendant problems of vibration and rapidity of motion)?

The more we talked about this the more excited we became. So we finished our work in Tijuana and returned home to call up the public relations department of the Goodyear company; and soon we were talking to Bob Masson, the public relations man in the Los Angeles office.

The Goodyear blimp.

It was quite apparent that Masson was intrigued with the idea; but he was also an employee of a very, very big corporation, and he had various people over him with whom he had to make contact. But the idea appealed to Bob, and it soon developed that he felt it *might* be possible to put it across.

There followed several days of telephone conversations. Then Bob came down to my ranch at Temecula, and after more telephone conversations with headquarters we worked out an arrangement.

The Goodyear people would furnish the blimp for four

days, April 17, 18, 19, and 20, weather permitting. There would be no advertising of any sort except the fact that the word GOODYEAR on the blimp was, of course, a permanent fixture. The object of the trip would be to give whatever publicity we could to the country and attempt to promote a better understanding of Baja California on the part of the people of the United States.

So we contacted Wulfrano Ruiz in Tijuana, Ricardo Castillo, and Alfredo López Gutiérrez, local head of the Tourist Bureau. We also contacted Rodolfo Valladolid, head of immigration for Baja California, and Licenciado Rafael Castillo Castro who was, at that time, an assistant mayor of Tijuana but who was promoted to the job of Secretario de Gobierno in La Paz while we were discussing plans.

I also got in touch with my friends Jack and Choral Pepper, the publisher and editor respectively of *Desert* magazine.

Desert magazine has included Baja California as part of the terrain in which it is interested, and the Peppers have been on several trips with me. They have found that their readers are tremendously interested in the peninsula, and Choral Pepper was enthusiastic in her endorsement of the idea and agreed to come along on the trip, the dates being such that Jack Pepper had to stay at the office.

It was then we began to find out some of the problems.

We have become so air-minded as a nation that we are prone to overlook the limitations of travel in lighter-than-air craft.

In the first place, there are various types of transportation in this class. There is the dirigible, which has a rigid frame. There is the balloon. And there is the blimp, which has no frame at all but simply a gas bag filled with a gas which makes it rise into the air.

This is in direct contradiction to the type of air thinking we have been accustomed to in the past few decades.

Wulfrano Ruiz and Choral Pepper.

With an airplane you are kept up in the air by the thrust of the motors and the airfoil of the wings. When anything happens to the motors, you go down.

With a dirigible your control is through the motors. If anything happens to your motors, you go up.

That's really an oversimplification, but it covers the general idea.

With a blimp there is no framework inside the bag. The bag is held distended by gas; in the case of the Goodyear balloon this is a helium gas, an inert gas which eliminates the danger of explosion.

This brings up a whole field of engineering problems.

As the blimp rises in the air the atmospheric pressure becomes less. Therefore the gas has a tendency to expand. If it expands enough, it is going to distend the blimp out of all shape, and it can conceivably burst the fabric.

Temperature is also quite a factor, as the gas has a tendency to expand as the weather gets warmer.

That sounds like an easy problem. Simply use less gas.

Remember, however, that it takes the gas pressure to hold

Sr. Rodolfo Valladolid, the Author, and Sr. Alfredo López Gutiérrez.

There is no framework inside the bag of the blimp.

The gondola seems very small.

the blimp in shape. The gondola is suspended from the blimp itself; and since the blimp has no framework, if there isn't enough pressure to hold the blimp in shape it is going to buckle in the middle—which will be disastrous to the occupants of the gondola.

The gondola of the blimp is designed to carry five passengers, a pilot, and a copilot. That's seven men all together, or, roughly speaking, a thousands pounds of live cargo. If the blimp is going to lift this live cargo, because the whole contraption is lighter than air, what is going to happen when

The motors must have enough thrust to bring the big dirigible back to the ground.

seven men get out of the blimp and the load is lightened by a thousand pounds?

Moreover, the blimp has to use gasoline motors, and gasoline motors consume gasoline. If you carry a hundred gallons of gasoline you have some six hundred pounds of fuel weight. What is going to happen when this fuel is consumed?

Furthermore, the blimp is a huge affair, a hundred and sixty-odd feet long and nearly sixty feet in height. It takes up a terrific amount of air space. If one has motors which are powerful enough to push this at any great rate of speed, the air resistance pyramids tremendously with each mile of speed obtained; as a result there is a critical speed which represents the maximum efficiency, one which will not consume too much gasoline, one which still will give the balloon reasonable headway.

When we started considering these problems we were amazed at the complications.

In order to control the gas pressure, the blimp has four flexible air tanks concealed in the bag. These tanks have intakes and vents. As the temperature gets higher, or as the blimp ascends, air must be let out of these air tanks so that the pressure within the bag does not become too great. Conversely, as the temperature lowers or the blimp descends in altitude, air must be taken into these collapsible bags so that the bag retains its shape and doesn't buckle in the middle under the weight of the gondola.

Quite obviously, with a gas bag of this size and all of its resulting air resistance, the rudders must be wide enough to make the big bag maneuverable. But here again we depend upon thrust and speed. If the motor dies, the gas bag simply drifts along with the wind like a piece of thistledown.

The idea is to have the combined weight of the fully loaded gondola on the ground so balanced that the whole weight is approximately twenty-five pounds, not more. Then the thrust of the motors can create enough air speed so that the rudders and vanes can elevate the bag to give it a good start. But as soon as the bag gets a start and gets higher, air must be released to compensate for the increased expansion of the helium gas.

Then, when it becomes necessary to bring the dirigible back to the ground, the motors must have enough thrust so that the air resistance on the elevators will send the blimp diving downward—despite the fact that owing to gasoline consumption it is considerably lighter than when it went up.

But how to hold it on the ground once it has been driven down by gasoline power is an entirely different question. It takes air resistance to actuate those vanes, and air resistance means speed through the air. Once the blimp becomes lighter than air it can't possibly stay on the ground without maintaining some speed.

Then, when the blimp gets onto the ground, the passengers want to disembark. Take a thousand pounds off the weight of the blimp and it is going to shoot up into the air.

Moreover, if a gust of wind comes scooting along the ground and the force of the air gets underneath the blimp just as a passenger is disembarking, it is conceivable that the bag will rise quite a few feet. A passenger climbing down the ladder, seeing the ground eighteen inches underneath, and preparing to take that last step, would be very much embarrassed to find that the distance to the ground had suddenly—just as he was putting his foot down—increased to twenty feet.

A solution to all of these problems is by no means simple.

Ropes are attached to the dirigible, great dangling ropes. A carefully trained ground crew of, I believe, eleven men grab the ropes and hold the blimp down whenever it descends.

These men travel in a big Greyhound-type bus. They must be in radio contact with the blimp at all times and be prepared to get under it whenever the blimp wants to come to earth. They not only have to hang onto the ropes, but they must have sandbags ready to hook onto the blimp to compensate for the weight of disembarking passengers. And then they have to hold the blimp on the ground until the new load of passengers gets aboard or until some thousand pounds of sandbags can be affixed to the blimp.

Furthermore, once the blimp gets onto the ground it becomes a huge weathervane. The nose is pointed into the wind. If the wind changes direction by just a few degrees, the whole blimp swings in a wide arc with the direction of the wind. With all of that air surface, the swing has terrific force.

Then there are still other problems. Turbulence in moun-

Bob Masson and Terry Elms.

tain areas causes the airplane to jump and buck like a rowboat in a choppy sea. What it does to a huge dirigible, with all of the area exposed to the air currents with a bag of that size and with no rigidity except what gas can give it, is something else again. And while the wings of an airplane tend to hold it rather flat in flight, the dirigible can and does develop a beautiful roll.

Bob Masson introduced us to Terry Elms, an animated young individual who is in charge of the highly specialized public relations for the dirigible itself, a man who is completely fascinated by the subject of lighter-than-air travel and who exudes statistics from his fingertips.

It soon became apparent that the critical top speed of the dirigible under ordinary conditions was thirty-five miles an hour, that for all practical purposes it had a height limit and it could not be taken over the high mountain ranges where we

Jean Bethell photographs our departure. Beside her is Bob Masson.

wanted it to go (between Tijuana and Mexicali), and that weather was a vital factor in the whole operation.

If one is traveling in a dirigible which has a top speed of thirty-five miles an hour and encounters a headwind of forty-five miles an hour, it is quite obvious that he is not only going nowhere fast, but that—if that wind is coming from the land and he has the open sea behind him—he is in a position which is somewhat less than enviable.

It is also apparent that if there should be any mix-up in signals and the ground crew should get lost, the dirigible might well be up there with no way of bringing it down to the ground—much less of holding it on the ground long enough to disembark the passengers.

And at this point I may state parenthetically that at one

time we did lose contact with our ground crew, and we were out over the wilds of Baja California—and it looked very much as if the ground crew had taken the wrong road and were hopelessly lost.

That was a thrill.

Of course, in places where the blimp is placed in normal use, the radio contacts are constant, and there are all kinds of emergency contacts which could be made in case of necessity. But down in Baja California, where one is out scouting over what is practically virgin terrain, a really close coordination becomes highly imperative: and the loss of contact presents quite a problem. I know that I sat up there for about an hour and a half while the blimp was cruising back and forth, the pilots frantically trying to get hold of the ground crew by radio with no success, and I wondered just what was going to happen. The gasoline consumption was making the blimp lighter all the time and, conceivably, if we ran out of gasoline we were just going to go drifting higher and higher and farther and farther, there being no way I know of to send a tow car for a disabled balloon.

While it had at first seemed easy to plan on getting to Tijuana and Ensenada, and then flying over the mountains to Mexicali, a summary of the conditions which we would encounter soon made it apparent that any idea of a trip to Mexicali was completely out of the question.

Even with favorable weather we would be lucky to complete our program in Tijuana and Ensenada.

Then there was the question of international complications. It turned out there were plenty of these. One doesn't simply send a huge dirigible over the international boundary line into Mexico without permission. There are, moreover, embargoes on taking helium out of the United States, and, in order to be on the safe side, it was necessary to have reserve supplies of helium. It was also rumored that under new mili-

The Goodyear blimp over Baja California.

tary restrictions it was illegal to photograph border cities from the air.

Then there was the question of getting permits from immigration. Quite obviously the ground crew going to work at this job were not tourists but laborers, and as such they needed some special dispensation. Furthermore, landing a huge dirigible at an airport takes up a large area, and arrangements had to be made for doing this.

In view of what has previously been mentioned, it is apparent that mooring the dirigible at night also presents a problem. Clearly, a group of men can't stand there holding ropes all night. Therefore a mooring mast has to be anchored with so many huge stakes that it can't possibly pull out. The bow of the blimp has to be moored to this mast. Then, as the wind changes, the tail swings back and forth. A hundred and seventy feet of dirigible could conceivably cover quite a circle.

We had discussed our planned trip with the Chambers of Commerce, the Tourist Bureau, the Mayors, and all the local officials in the border cities, and found they were all enthusiastic in their cooperation. They started telephoning Mexico City for official governmental sanction, while the Goodyear Tire and Rubber Company, in turn, was putting pressure to bear on Washington. Washington was communicating with the American Embassy in Mexico City.

Time was very, very short, and in all probability we received the fastest official international cooperation that has ever been achieved. Even so, our last permission wasn't granted in Mexico City until Friday, April 14, and the company telephoned Bob Masson in Los Angeles that everything was now in order and the permit was being sent airmail special delivery.

Then minor problems arose.

The blimp is arranged so that illuminated night messages in letters ten feet high can be sent streaming across the full length of the big gas bag, the only limitation being that no one word can contain more than ten letters.

Since we were determined that we were going to have no advertising of any sort—either for Goodyear, *Desert* magazine, or Gardner—we wanted to use this spectacular nighttime display of lettering to convey messages of friendship. However, these messages necessarily had to be in Spanish and we had, so to speak, to teach the blimp how to speak in Spanish.

Then came the question of weather.

April of 1967 in Southern California was a particularly wild and unruly month, with rainstorm after rainstorm lashing the coast, high winds, clouds, and, for Southern California, what was bitterly cold weather.

All of which brought up another question, which was that the cabin of the blimp had no heat of any sort. When we got

Passengers in the gondola take the weather as they find it.

up in that gondola we would be facing whatever type of weather was going to be hurled at us, and we were advised to bring warm clothes and plenty of warm drinks in thermos bottles. In short, the blimp was not primarily designed for cross-country travel. It was designed to take passengers up over a city on short goodwill trips or to give important personages the thrill of going up in a blimp. It was also designed to cover certain important events by television. It was not intended for the use we were going to make of it.

We were giving the blimp a brand-new concept in using it to improve international friendship, and we were subjecting ourselves to quite an experiment.

Just how experimental it was can be determined by the fact that, when we returned, the company officially notified us that Wulfrano Ruiz and I had had more passenger hours in the blimp than any two men in history.

As time grew shorter we prayed for good weather, and when the weather forecast for Monday, April 17, was for high winds and showers, we almost gave up. However, we kept in telephone communication and decided to take everything in stride and not to throw in the towel as long as there was any possibility of making the flight.

5

Weather Permitting

My executive secretary Jean Bethell, her sister Peggy Downs (who keeps all of the names and files at her fingertips)—two of the three sisters who have been with me as secretaries for many years—Sam Hicks, and I got up a little before five o'clock Monday morning and wakened Choral Pepper, who had driven over from Palm Springs the night before.

We hoped there would be time for breakfast in San Diego.

We drove down to the field in San Diego where the Goodyear people said a plane would pick us up at seven-fifteen.

I, for one, felt absolutely certain the plane would be delayed for one reason or another, and we would have ample time for at least a hurried breakfast at the airport.

We arrived at San Diego about fifteen minutes ahead of schedule and were met by Wulfrano Ruiz, Ricardo Castillo, Alfonso Martínez (nicknamed "Pluma Blanca"), and Capitán Francisco Muñoz, the veteran airplane pilot who does all of my flying south of the border.

To our surprise we found the plane was ready and waiting, and we climbed aboard the Goodyear *Executive Lodestar*, taxied down the field, and were soon in the air headed for Los Angeles.

Wulfrano Ruiz being interviewed for television.

The weather was not as bad as the forecaster had predicted, nor was it as good as we could have wished, but at this point we were taking the trip one step at a time.

We landed in Los Angeles and found the Goodyear company had two limousines there to meet us. We were transported to the grounds where the blimp was kept and then learned that several television stations had become intrigued with the idea of our trip to Baja California and wanted interviews. So our departure was delayed while we were interrogated about the purpose of the trip, our views on international relations, and all of the hundred-and-one questions which popped up in the minds of the interviewers.

We also learned that United Press International wanted to send a photographer along to cover the entire expedition, and Carlos Schiebeck was waiting with an assortment of various cameras draped around his neck and shoulders. Here also we

The Author and Carlos Schiebeck, the United Press photographer.

learned that, because of the weight of gasoline required, it would be impossible to take more than two passengers in addition to the pilot, the copilot, and the UPI photographer. Since we all wanted as much coverage as possible, we agreed that the photographer was an essential part of the organization. In fact, before we got done we had adopted Carlos into the family, and he proved not only an exceptionally fine photographer but also a wonderful companion.

So Wulfrano Ruiz and I climbed aboard the blimp. I confess I had a little trepidation. That gondola looked very thin and flimsy underneath the huge towering bag which swayed in the breeze above us.

The motors were started. The men got on the ropes. The blimp was lifted slightly, then lowered abruptly, and the takeoff came on the bounce.

When an airplane is put into too steep a climb there is

The Balboa Yacht Club at Balboa Beach.

always the danger of a stall. However, you can't stall a blimp, and I was surprised at the rate of climb. They put the nose up into the air, stood the blimp almost on its tail, and we went away from there fast.

This was a real thrill, sitting in a gondola with wide windows, no wings to obstruct our vision, watching the country as it drifted slowly by, having an opportunity to study people and places.

In an airplane one has a fleeting glimpse of a house, then it is left behind. One sees a car speeding along a highway, and within a few seconds it too has vanished.

In a blimp, however, the situation is different. You drift along looking out of the wide windows at the houses beneath, picking out some particular person who is doing something in a yard, wondering about the people who live in a particular building.

You become interested in a particular car which is threading its way through traffic, going in the same direction the blimp is going, and you follow its progress for minute after minute.

Blimping is different from any other type of transportation I have ever experienced, and Wulfrano Ruiz and I were completely fascinated.

In all my experience there has been nothing quite like that of riding in a blimp.

Just as riding in a sailboat, moving silently with a breeze along the surface of the water, is entirely different from being in a power cruiser, so is riding in a blimp different from cruising in an airplane or a helicopter.

I have never had the experience of riding in a glider, but I understand that this also is utterly unlike any other form of air transportation.

I think probably much of the sensation of flying in a glider is experienced by passengers in a blimp.

In a helicopter I always feel that I am in a big soap bubble. I look down between my feet and see the terrain two or three thousand feet below, look around within the comparatively narrow confines of the plastic shell, and sometimes have the feeling that the bubble is about to burst.

While there are gasoline motors to furnish motive power for the blimp, the displacement of the gas bag is such that little would be gained by adding a greater power thrust. Therefore, the motors are relatively small, just big enough to give sufficient headway to furnish a means of control and to move from point to point.

Instead of the soap-bubble image I get in a helicopter, in a blimp I have the feeling of being a spider riding a spider balloon.

I think we have all seen these spider balloons.

A certain type of spider sits on a twig at the end of a limb and spins a long, gossamer streamer of web which floats out into the breeze. As this web gets big enough, it becomes a species of sail or parachute. The spider is then literally pulled off the twig and taken for a long ride until he comes down in a new environment.

Why do spiders do this?

We say it is instinct.

What instinct? Why? What is the spider trying to accomplish? Or, to put it another way, what is nature trying to accomplish by sending these spiders out searching for new terrain?

Probably the spiders feed upon insects which are destructive to crops; and nature, always searching for a balance, gives the insects the power to propagate and distribute themselves, and then, in turn, wants the spiders to cover as much territory as possible.

I have seen these spiders by the hundreds, drifting out across the open water in the Delta region of the Sacramento, San Joaquin, and Mokelumne rivers. Untold thousands of the poor things are condemned to a watery death. But occasionally one of them will land on our houseboat, promptly proceed to cut himself loose from his gossamer balloon, and take up residence with us.

The fact that the spiders spin these balloons where only water can be seen means that they are acting purely from instinct, with no conscious determination as to where they are going. Nature gives them the urge to travel, and the fact that they are traveling to their death is immaterial. A few thousand of the spiders are sacrificed in order that the plan of nature may go on.

Everywhere, we see that the life of the individual is unimportant compared with the master plan of nature.

However, while I realize that as an individual I am unimportant compared with nature's over-all plan, I am enough of

We cruise over a marina.

an individual so that I have a certain regard for my own safety.

Perhaps this also is merely a phase of nature's plan. The individual is given the instinct to survive so that the race may survive. It is just possible that if the individual could see, back of the veil, the peace, the harmony, and the eternal justice of the divine pattern of perpetual life, he would be less resistant to the experience which we refer to as death.

And since this would violate nature's plan, which is to have the various species survive against all odds, nature decrees that the individual must, therefore, be conscious of only one phase of existence at a time and have no definite knowledge of the pattern of life throughout eternity.

I had some of these thoughts as I sat in the gondola of the blimp when it started cruising along the coast, then out over the water, settling down to a mere two hundred and fifty feet above the ocean as we glided along the shore.

Wulfrano Ruiz reacting to a sonic boom hitting the blimp.

I looked around the gondola. I knew it was fastened to the gas bag by ropes. How firmly were those ropes secured? What were the chances of breakage?

As I was wondering about this, suddenly the whole gondola shivered and shook. It felt as though every rope had parted simultaneously.

I saw the pilots come up out of their seats a fraction of an inch. I came up out of my seat a good eighteen inches.

Somebody laughed.

They knew what I was thinking. They turned and one of them explained, "We have been hit by a sonic boom."

That's what it had been, all right, but it had certainly scared me, and I have a feeling it gave just a little, tiny, teensy bit of a momentary scare to the pilot and copilot.

For some ten days Wulfrano Ruiz had been working his head off, getting things lined up so that we could have an official welcome at both Tijuana and Ensenada. And here I want to express my appreciation for the loyalty of the Mexicans who promised they would be on hand to receive us. As it turned out we were nearly two and a half hours overdue when we landed at Tijuana. But the Mayor, the various officials, and hundreds of the citizens were there to meet us with official courtesies, to give us a key to the city and a warm handclasp of welcome.

Our blimp had quite a problem. We had to keep in touch with the ground crew all the way. We had to fight a headwind. We had to try to maintain our schedule.

Bob Masson had prepared a very appetizing lunch for us. In the mad scramble of departure we had left it behind. Bob radioed us about it, but we simply didn't have time to go back and pick it up.

So Wulfrano Ruiz and I, without breakfast, were marooned in the blimp with no chance of getting lunch.

The ground crew had a chance to get far enough ahead of us to stop off for a quick bite, but we slogged along in the blimp, gliding slowly over the coast.

There are, I believe, regulations which cover the height at which a blimp may navigate over cities, but over the ocean it can go to any elevation the pilot chooses. So we got out over the water and went down the coast, flying at about two hundred and fifty feet, giving us a chance to see all of the beach cities.

I was astonished at the development of these cities. It is getting so that one almost joins the other; and the increase in enthusiasm for boating was quite manifest because many new marinas have been constructed since I last had an opportunity to view the coastline.

Here I had a chance to observe an ingenious procedure by which the navigators get the actual ground speed of the blimp.

Timing the shadow of the dirigible to ascertain its speed.

They time the shadow!

They fly so the shadow of the blimp glides smoothly over the land. They pick out a landmark—a tree, a rock, or a building—and when the shadow of the blimp's nose first touches that landmark the pilots press the button on a stopwatch.

When the tail part of the shadow passes the landmark, the stopwatch gives the time in seconds and fractions of a second.

Since the exact length of the dirigible is known, it is possible to get the exact ground speed, which, with only a fairly gentle headwind, may be less than twenty-five miles an hour.

We were so busy taking pictures and so excited that we hardly realized the lapse of time, despite the fact my stomach was busy sending telegraphic messages to my brain that something very serious had been overlooked. It is interesting that the stomach and the brain never lose radio contact.

Eventually we turned inland and came to Montgomery

Alfonso Martínez and Ricardo Castillo wait for me to board the blimp at Montgomery Field. Choral Pepper is already seated in the gondola. Note the "sand bags," filled with lead shot, which hold the blimp on the ground.

Field, where we had some delay getting the ground crew on the job. Then we landed, and by this time the load had been lightened enough so that Choral Pepper and Jean Bethell could ride with us over to Tijuana.

The Goodyear executive plane had flown our group back to San Diego, buzzing the blimp en route. They had picked up the automobiles left at the airport, transferred them to Montgomery Field, and were ready to precede us into Tijuana.

Once again we were in the air, this time flying at a considerable elevation due to navigational restrictions.

The weather was still fairly clear, but rain and winds were expected over the next few days and there was a cold wind. The temperature in the gondola was rather low for comfort.

We sailed smoothly southward, crossed the border, and started circling over Tijuana, waiting for the ground crew to

Tijuana.

get through customs and immigration, getting tourist permits for all of the members.

The Mexican officials did everything they could to expedite matters, but with one thing and another we were very badly overdue when we finally came to the Tijuana airport and got the ground crew on the job after we had circled repeatedly.

We had quite a greeting.

The Mayor of Tijuana, Francisco López Gutiérrez, presented us with a parchment making us distinguished guests of Tijuana and gave us a gold key to the city. A group of charros, the handsome Mexican riders, were there with their big sombreros, and one of the men, Roberto de la Madrid, presented me with his own tightly woven poncho blanket with silver buttons.

We were presented with a beautiful oil painting of the Misión de San Fernando de Valicata, executed by the famous artist John Dingler Alva, who expressed his pleasure that we

The Jai-alai Building in Tijuana.

could have one of his works. There was a jade-and-gold inlaid plaque, and above all, an atmosphere of cordial welcome.

Many prominent people were there; the consuls of several countries: Ruben D. Luna of San Salvador, Hans G. Holt-schmit O. of Germany, Maxine Argoud of France, General Servando Osornio of Belgium, Arturo Olivieri of Italy and John R. Bartlett from the United States. There were city, state, and federal officials, and a great mass of curious spectators. The crowd was so dense we couldn't get good pictures of the reception.

Within the course of a few minutes we had more gifts, more honors, and had experienced more genuine downright hospitality than could possibly have been expected.

Then the blimp pilots started taking up a few very important people. The Mayor was of course passenger number one, followed by several of the top executives and various officials.

At this time I want to pay my respects to The Honorable

Left to right: Wulfrano Ruiz, Capitán Francisco Muñoz, the Honorable Francisco López Gutiérrez, the Author, Alfonso Martínez, and Oswaldo Castillo.

Francisco López Gutiérrez, Mayor of Tijuana. I have met him on several occasions and I am tremendously impressed by him as a man, an executive, and a statesman. He is conscientious but broadminded. He is determined to end graft, to control vice, and to stamp out corruption. I predict that within a few years Tijuana *will* have a new image, a fascinating image which will cause tourists to stay much longer than the average time now spent in the city by visitors; and along with this new image will come a fantastic prosperity.

We watched the big blimp go up and circle the city, were on hand to greet the party when it descended, and then started for the motor hotel, The Hotel Country Club a relatively new and wonderfully fine hostelry across from the racetrack.

Here rooms had been reserved for us, and I relaxed in comfort for half an hour before having a 6:30 P.M. breakfast and lunch combined.

Then we went to a cocktail party at the Chamber of Commerce.

I had understood this was to be only cocktails and didn't know they had a buffet supper as well. So while the food was a long time in coming that day, when it did come it came all at once.

On the blimp trip, however, my stomach had to learn to store food as the camel's stomach stores water.

We were usually up and around too early for any breakfast except a hasty cup of coffee. Then we were up in the blimp, and the mechanics of blimping are such that the ground crew can eat only when the blimp is in the air or when it is moored to a mast on the ground. This is because it takes a full complement of men and sandbags to hold the blimp on the ground when there is even a moderate breeze blowing. And that blimp is like a multimillion-dollar baby. It has to be guarded at all times.

So we would usually be cruising while the ground crew was eating lunch. Then we would wait for the ground crew to catch up with us, and by that time dinner would be in order.

The meeting that night at the Chamber of Commerce was really thrilling. The assembly room was packed, and officials and other speakers extended their friendship in both Spanish and English.

Following the buffet dinner there was an executive conference. President Gustavo Díaz Ordaz of Mexico was due in

Exterior view of the Tijuana Hotel.

Tijuana in a week, and it was earnestly desired to have the blimp cruising over Tijuana with illuminated messages honoring the President and expressing international goodwill.

We knew that this would be no easy task on such short notice, but we discussed ways and means, and blocked out wires we would send to the executives of the Goodyear Tire and Rubber Company.

Bob Masson and Terry Elms thought we just might be able to get a favorable reply by burning up the wires in appeals to key executives.*

---

* The Goodyear Tire and Rubber Company got busy and cut all red tape. When the President of Mexico reached Tijuana the blimp was there, floating over the night sky with its illuminated messages of welcome—a remarkably impressive sight.

6

On to Ensenada

Tuesday morning was devoted to taking up as many of the important people in Tijuana as could possibly be accommodated. We again missed lunch because we were so busy. This day, however, we were not quite so starved. We had learned to eat big breakfasts. We had had breakfast with Ricardo, whose restaurant furnishes a breakfast which will, I believe, enable anybody to last until night without thinking about anything more to eat.

Ricardo takes papaya, strawberries, oranges and orange juice, sometimes a little pineapple, and blends these ingredients in a high-speed blender until it is a thick fruit compote. This concoction is remarkably soothing to the fuzzy-tongued condition which sometimes follows a late night.

Then there are eggs, platters of refried beans, tortillas, savory pork chops which are cooked in some sort of delightful sweet-and-sour barbecue sauce, and great quantities of fresh tropical fruits.

Ricardo is a wonderful manager. He has lithe, attractive girls who wait on tables in the restaurant with eager alacrity, a bright-eyed anticipation of the wants of the customer, and

Professor Jorge Olguín Hermida, Mayor of Ensenada.

instantaneous execution which makes the food even more palatable.

And then at about two o'clock we took off in the blimp for Ensenada. It was a beautiful trip down the coast. The shoreline of this portion of Mexico presents one of the most perfect examples of marine scenery to be found anywhere in the West. Whereas the ocean-frontage land in the United States is crowded to capacity, there are some wonderfully beautiful spots all along the sixty-odd miles of coast between Tijuana and Ensenada which are still being farmed as acreage.

Our arrival in Ensenada was again the signal for quite a demonstration.

The Mayor, Professor Jorge Olguín Hermida, was there with a gold key to the city, with plaques, presents, and speeches. After an on-the-spot reception, a few of the promi-

Rugged coastline. (Note the ropes hanging from the blimp.)

nent Ensenada people were taken up in the blimp, which later on was moored to the mast for the night.

The ground crew had done a terrific job pulling up the mooring mast, getting their equipment loaded, driving all the way down the coast keeping the blimp in sight, then arriving in Ensenada and putting up the mast for the night mooring. Our ground speed in the blimp had been reduced to eighteen

Our arrival at Ensenada.

miles an hour due to headwinds, and this had complicated the problem of the ground crew.

Again that night we had a wonderful ceremony; during a banquet hosted by the Tourist Bureau I was presented with several objects of art, including a beautifully engraved plaque carrying the superbly done head of a Mayan warrior.

Just after breakfast the next morning my esteemed friend, General Carlos Reyes Aviles, came to the hotel to greet me.

Twenty-odd years ago, when I made my first trip to Baja California, General Reyes Aviles was the general in charge of the district. Together with our companions we called on him to pay our respects and ask for his cooperation.

We were so impressed with the courtesy of our reception that we later sent General Reyes Aviles books from time to time, and we were soon exchanging cards at Christmas.

The years passed; General Reyes Aviles retired, but he remained an important and powerful personage in Baja California.

Now I was thrilled to have this courteous gentleman, with his erect military bearing, come to the hotel to greet me as an old friend.

Bless his soul, he is the personification of the true Mexican gentleman, and he is a wonderful and loyal friend.

While in Ensenada we had the pleasure of an audience with General Cruz Calvo and Lieutenant Colonel Federico A.

Left to right: The Author, General Carlos Reyes Aviles, his grandson, and Ricardo Castillo.

General Cruz Calvo, the Author, and Col. Federico A. Espinosa de los Monteros.

Espinosa de los Monteros. It happened that on my first trip down Baja California Colonel Espinosa had acted as interpreter when we had called on General Reyes Aviles. Now it was a pleasure to meet this splendid officer again as he acted as interpreter for General Cruz Calvo. We had a very enjoyable visit.

That morning we again had rides for important people in Ensenada, and then we took off on a trip of exploration—Choral Pepper, Sam Hicks, Wulfrano Ruiz, Ricardo Castillo, and I.

We went down to the blowhole—one of nature's phenomena—which is beautiful from the air, but not nearly as impressive as when one stands on the ground and watches the foamy mass of salt water exploding into the air high above the heads of spectators.

In the blimp, however, we were able to observe the turbulent nature of the ocean at this point and to see the beautiful coloring of the water and white surf.

Then we took more pictures of Ensenada and went into the back country.

This was the best part of the journey to me because I had long wanted to explore this area.

The landscape was beautiful at this time of year. There had been rains, the grass was green, and the hill slopes were car-

The blowhole below Ensenada.

The blimp over Ensenada heads for the beautiful bay of Todos Santos and its protected anchorage.

The business center of Ensenada.

peted with a green mantle. However, it was unfortunate from a standpoint of black-and-white photography, because green photographs as black and it was not possible to get really good pictures for reproduction.

Nevertheless, we studied the terrain at various elevations and in different parts of the back country. In this way I was able to get a much clearer picture than I had ever been able to get from airplanes or from the four-wheel-drive explorations I had made on previous trips.

We had hoped to get out as far as the Meling Ranch, but with headwinds and the fact that we had a late start we realized we couldn't possibly make it.

The Melings have long been in the country and have a ranch where they take paying guests, where one can hunt both big and small game, ride horses, inhale the crystal-pure air on the slope of the San Pedro Mártir range, and generally relax.

They are wonderfully pleasant, hospitable people who have the knack of making the visitor feel at home. We had previously visited their ranch by air, coming down on a good landing strip, and I was hoping that we could get out there with the blimp. But there were just so many things to do we never did have time to get caught up with our schedule.

We returned after zigzagging around the mountains, and reached the field in Ensenada just as the sun was setting.

The ground crew moored the blimp to the mast and we went to a beautiful dinner at the Hotel Bahía where my friend Ing. Felipe de J. Ricalde Lugo, who is the head of the Ensenada Tourist Bureau in Ensenada and who is also the manager of the hotel, made us welcome.

That night after dinner the blimp glided slowly over Ensenada, with great ten-foot-high electric signs along the sides conveying a message of friendship.

No one wanted to go to bed. The pilots of the blimp, and

the public relations men from Goodyear, our Mexican friends, and our party were becoming cemented into a big, warm family.

The Hotel Bahía has an excellent and very typically Mexican floor show reminiscent of the history of the country. We enjoyed the floor show. We enjoyed our friendships.

Victor Corral and his wife joined us, two longtime friends.

Corral was for years Francisco Muñoz's chief assistant in the piloting field, and we have flown many, many hours with him over Baja California, having many an adventure together. It was a pleasure to be with them.

Even when the hour became quite late we didn't want to break up the party; but gradually we began to feel the aftermath of all the excitement and, at the very late hour of midnight, we retired to a sleep of peaceful oblivion.

The next day we had a big job ahead of us. We started early from Ensenada and embarked upon what was intended to be the highlight of the trip.

Ranch houses in Baja California.

Jean Bethell, Ricardo Castillo, and Peggy Downs in front of the Bahía Hotel at Ensenada.

When I had been exploring Baja California by helicopter we had made it a point to circle over some interesting ranch and, if we had welcoming smiles from the inhabitants, we'd drop down to a landing, get acquainted, and perhaps take the head of the family up for a ride in one of the helicopters—giving him an eye-popping adventure and leaving him with something to tell his grandchildren.

Somebody said why not do the same thing with a blimp?

I looked up in astonishment.

It is one thing to land a helicopter in somebody's backyard. It is quite another thing to bring a hundred-and-sixty-seven-foot dirigible balloon out of the sky. You must find a place where it can be moored without entangling itself in barbed-wire fences and where there is room to swing, so that the changing wind will not cause the tail assembly to get fouled in some thorn-covered tree. And it is hardly feasible to have eight or ten men sitting on ropes while one gets acquainted with the owner of a ranch.

However, it was an adventure, and we wanted adventure—so up we went.

I said that we wanted adventure—adventure we had.

It was felt that it might take some time for us to locate a suitable ranch, so it was decided that the blimp would start exploring and then keep in touch with the ground crew by radio. When we had found a ranch the ground crew could, at least theoretically, see us high in the sky, drive directly into the vicinity, and receive more detailed radio instructions from the air.

So we started blissfully along, leaving the ground crew to pull up the mooring mast, break it into its component parts, get them all loaded, and then get the personnel in the bus and station wagon. Sam and our group were to follow in our station wagon, while Ricardo was to drive Victor Corral's car. Victor was to give us his knowledge of the country so that we wouldn't get lost.

The blimp over Ensenada.

Those were the plans.

So we carefully followed a map Victor Corral had made, went through the valley to Guadalupe, then on into the mountains, circling around looking for a ranch that offered the right possibilities.

We found one and circled and circled, finally giving up as we realized that no one was home.

It then became necessary to find an alternate ranch.

By this time, however, a very serious situation had developed. It appeared that we were lost, or, rather, that the ground crew was lost.

The time when they were to report from directly underneath us had long since passed.

So we started circling on a back track, looking for the huge bus with its telltale yellow sides and the word "Goodyear" printed on them.

We also instituted a search by radio.

We got nowhere with either search.

Hours had passed since we took off from Ensenada, and I had visions of being marooned in a blimp.

We had pulled stakes in Ensenada and were on our way to the border. If they lost us, would the ground crew go to

School children running out to see the blimp as we cruise above Guadalupe.

Tijuana to look for us, or would they spend the night in a frantic search of the mountain country trying to pick up a radio signal?

So much for the ground crew. What would we be doing?

Being up in a blimp with no ground crew to bring the big bag in to a landing is no situation to be casually brushed to one side.

The engines and the elevators can force the bag down to the ground, but it takes a certain velocity to get enough air pressure on the elevators to bring the bag down. Once it is down it has to keep moving to stay down, unless there are people to pull on ropes and other people to hook on sandbags filled with ballast.

And the longer the blimp is in the air with the motors running the more gasoline is used, and the more gasoline used the lighter the weight.

I began to get all sorts of thoughts.

Had the ground crew gone up the wrong road, or had they been in a car wreck?

As nearly as I could tell it had to be one or the other.

In the meantime we had open ocean to the west and high jagged mountains to the east; and Baja California is noted for its sudden violent windstorms, with winds sometimes reaching ninety miles an hour—our top speed was about a third of that. A high wind from either the east or the west could well have been disastrous.

Finally we decided to forget all about landing at a ranch and try instead to locate the ground crew. So we started back along the road to Ensenada, anxiously searching the highway with binoculars, continually probing with our radio.

I learned afterward that our radio messages had been received during all this time by the ground crew, which had been desperately trying to reply. But owing to the fact that we were confronted with good clear sending conditions while the car was hampered with natural obstacles on the terrain, we never received their reply. But finally we established radio contact—almost at the same moment we spotted the bus on the highway.

The ground crew's trouble with the mooring mast had resulted in a long delay, and they couldn't reach us by radio to tell us what had gone wrong.

It was now getting well along in the afternoon. We were out in a rolling country with a range of mountains between us and Tijuana, where we had to be that night. A fresh breeze had started up, and the pilots warned us there would be turbulence when we tried to cross the mountain range.

However, encouraged by the presence of the ground crew, we decided to touch down at one of the ranches because it would be so interesting to see the reaction of the people when a giant balloon started to park in their front yard.

We finally located a ranch where someone seemed to be home, and circled the house. Dogs ran out and started a frenzied barking. People stared up at us in stupefied amazement.

We gave directions to the cars, and the ground crew started over what from the air seemed to be a very beautiful dirt road.

We try to land at a ranch.

Actually the road consisted of ruts with high centers, and very shortly the big bus found itself marooned on a high center with all four wheels off the ground, as helpless as a ship stranded high and dry on a reef.

We circled and circled and circled.

Down below men and dogs began to appear from nowhere. The family in the little ranch house came out to get under the blimp, staring up at us with open-mouthed awe.

Finally the crowd got the bus back into operation. The ground crew ran out into a field. The wind was now blowing hard and the pilots brought the blimp in to a landing after some difficulty.

Personally, I doubt if we could have held the blimp with the ground crew we had, but by this time people were coming from all over. Cars stopped along the road and we had a horde of volunteers on the ropes—and we needed them. When I got out, the wind was much stronger than I had anticipated.

I say that people had appeared from nowhere, but they were not the only audience. Dogs came from neighboring ranch houses, from as far away as they could hear the excited yapping of the local dogs. This was the biggest game they had ever chased, and all of the men in the community were not only helping them chase it but were holding it down with ropes so it couldn't get away, and some of the dogs tried to grab hold of a rope with their teeth and help. Failing in this, they barked hysterical delight at being permitted to engage in such a mighty hunt.

These people at the ranch on which we landed were well nourished. As far as the products of the land were concerned, they had plenty. It was only in their clothing, where the dollars began to enter into the picture, that their lack of wealth was manifest.

I was pleased to note, however, that their dogs were in

superb condition and quite evidently well fed and happy.

Despite the fact that there were five or six heavy men on each of the ropes, men hanging onto the fuselage, and sandbags dangling, the wind was whipping the blimp around so that our visit on the ground consisted of little more than shaking hands, having pictures taken, and again climbing back into the blimp to head for Tijuana.

The pilots had been right about turbulence in the mountains. The blimp reacts in a peculiar way to turbulence and develops a rolling motion, which is a new experience for me in air travel.

The blimp is almost sixty feet high, which means that the gondola is suspended thirty feet below the center of gravity. Swinging back and forth over mountains at the end of a thirty-four-foot pendulum, and at the same time going up and down, gives the passenger a somewhat queasy sensation.

People come rushing from all directions to pull on the ropes as the family comes out to meet us.

The huge bullfighting ring in Tijuana.

We reached Tijuana, circled the city for some two and a
half hours waiting for the ground crew, then descended and
went at once to the Hotel Country Club, where again I had
an hour's rest before we went to the Palermo Restaurant for
dinner.

The Palermo Restaurant, operated by Tony Busterno, is a
remarkably fine restaurant with an Italian motif, but delicious
food of all kinds can be obtained.

Not only is Tony a great friend, but his chief waiter, Oscar,
is also a longtime friend of mine who sees that all of my wants
are taken care of.

That evening was one long to be remembered.

By this time all of the strangeness had worn off, and those of
us involved in the blimp project had become accustomed to
each other's companionship. Moreover, Wulfrano Ruiz's wife
came to join us. Terry Elms, the young man who has charge
of publicity pertaining to the blimp, brought a young woman

friend of his from San Diego. The pilots of the blimp came in, headed by Roy Belotti, the captain. And, in addition, there were local friends who dropped in to join us.

Oscar had started out with a table for eight, tastefully set in a choice location. Soon he made it a table for ten. Then he added another table, then another table, and finally still a third table.

Oscar took it all in his stride, however. The bartender kept mixing the drinks and Oscar kept serving them. Then, when it came time for food, Oscar somehow managed to get everyone served while the food was hot.

Our trip down Baja California had been exhausting in many ways, and I think everyone there needed rest. Yet we all hated to break up the party. Sometime after midnight, however, it became necessary to leave because the ground crew had already taken the blimp across to San Diego, and they had a long drive across the border to their night quarters.

The next day I was scheduled to be on the NBC program, "*Today*," which was being taped aboard a landing craft out in the San Diego harbor.

Bob Masson and Sam Hicks at the Tijuana Airport.

The idea was that the cameras could pick up San Diego in the background and show the beautiful city—with the shore-line, skyscrapers, the distant mountains basking in the sunlight.

Terry Elms arranged to have the blimp cruise back and forth, so that when I told of returning from my blimp trip the television cameras could look up and catch the blimp.

Weather permitting.

The correspondence I had had with Bob Masson and Terry Elms always emphasized the fact that all plans in connection with the blimp were predicated upon the two words, "Weather permitting."

We got up in Tijuana on that Friday morning and went to Ricardo's for breakfast, where we were joined by Ricardo's wife, Graciela, and Alfonso Martínez and his wife and boy.

Again we had one of Ricardo's breakfasts which would keep a lumberjack going all day; and because three days of blimping had made me learn that you take food when and if you can get it, I really stocked up on food.

Then we said farewell with lots of good old-fashioned Mexican *abrazos*, which is a form of expressing affection for close friends, and then we were on our way across the border into San Diego.

The sky was overcast, and it rapidly became more overcast. A cold icy wind came hurling down out of the northwest. Rain began to fall.

Overhead we could see the blimp bravely battling the elements so that the company could be true to its promise to have the blimp available.

Alas for the idea of showing sun-swept San Diego in the television cameras!

Our alert lieutenant commander was waiting with the gig. We climbed aboard and buffeted our way out to the landing craft, and were ushered into a small but warm stateroom. In

Aerial view of the country between Ensenada and Tijuana.

due course, I went out onto the windswept deck where Hugh
Downs, bundled up as though he were facing an arctic storm,
was conducting the interviews in front of the television
cameras.

We got through with the interview and then managed to
get into the gig—or whatever it is they call it; I am a confirmed landlubber—and reached shore in the middle of the
coldest, most windy, most disagreeable, most rain-spattered

April I have ever remembered in all my years spent in Southern California.

However, we had made the blimp trip. Weather had permitted, and we had carried out our schedule.

I had seen some interesting country that I wanted to explore, and I had confirmed my impression that there in the back country there are miles of brush-covered hills with grassy open spaces where one can see the game trails almost as if the country had been used to pasture sheep.

We had had a heartwarming experience of greeting old friends and making new ones. We had participated in one of the most dramatic gestures of international friendship and understanding that had ever been undertaken by the Goodyear Tire and Rubber Company.

And the men who were on the blimp and on the landing crew had had their eyes opened to a new aspect of Mexico.

As Terry Elms told me, "I have been to Tijuana several times. If anybody asked me if I knew Tijuana I would have said, 'Why, certainly, I have been there and have been all over it.' Now I have seen a side of Tijuana I never knew existed. I have seen things in Tijuana and in Ensenada which have given me an honest and deep admiration for the Mexicans. I have seen a side of the Mexican character which I knew nothing about before I made this trip."

And it was apparent that many of those other men had a new perspective on Mexico.

For instance, when the ground crew had knocked off for lunch in Ensenada and gone dashing down the road, looking for a place to grab a quick sandwich, they had found a nice-looking drive-in restaurant, had parked the cars, and had gone inside and sat at the counter.

It happened they caught the little restaurant flat-footed, and with sixteen hungry men walking in and wanting food quickly there was a delay, a very serious delay.

Jesús Pineda Nuñez, right, and his assistant, Manuela Rodríguez, invite the ground crew for a dinner "on the house."

Eventually the men got their food and returned to the field.

Late that afternoon the proprietor of the restaurant drove up. He had just heard about the delay and its serious consequences. He was very, very sorry. Would the ground crew let him make atonement by taking them all out to dinner that night at his expense?

The ground crew felt somewhat embarrassed, but thinking that the man might have been insulted if his invitation had been declined, they accepted; and that night they had a bounteous repast as the guests of a restaurant proprietor whom they had never seen before.

Things of this sort are quite typical of the Mexican character if one is only willing to keep an open mind, to observe and be courteous.

I returned to find my desk piled high with letters which had accumulated in my absence. I was impatient to dispose of them as soon as possible so that we could once more get started exploring the back country—some of which we had seen from the blimp, some of which we had seen only as the purple outlines of mountain peaks against the western sky when we had camped in the land of the PaiPai Indians.

Carlos Schiebeck, of United Press International, had taken hundreds of pictures. He wanted to be sure he had the names correct in the captions, and it was arranged that Terry Elms, Carlos Schiebeck, and Ricardo would meet at our ranch the following Thursday for a barbecue. And then, just as soon as we could get our outfit together, we wanted to get Pappy Hazard and take our four-wheel-drive cars out for further exploration.

By this time I realized that the story of Mexico's Magic Square could only be hinted at in one book and there is just too much material available to be covered by a single individual. But I decided to do the best I could to explore the backbone of the Sierra de Juárez, pause for a further look at Mexicali, and then move on down to San Felipe to investigate some of the country between San Felipe and Laguna Salada.

7

The Woodcutters

When I explore in Mexico I like to have someone with me who has firsthand familiarity with the country, insofar as this is possible. Of course, with our helicopter explorations we get into country which is virtually virgin territory, and here it is impossible to have guides in the ordinary sense of the word. But when we travel with our four-wheel-drive vehicles, we not only like to have people who can help with the driving and camp work but who can also speak the language fluently and are *simpático*.

In this way we give work to Mexicans who need the money. We enlarge our circle of acquaintances. We are able to enjoy life to better advantage, and we have a lot more downright fun.

Perhaps that is part of the experience of camping which I enjoy so much. The smell of wood smoke, the fact that we can take life easy so that there is always the sound of laughter; and we give work to men who need work, always at a wage that is just above the going rate so that they are happy in their work.

When we come to the little ranches we can stop and visit,

130

not as tourists going through the country, but as a group of
people who have things in common with the ranchers and
who can provide a welcome break in the monotony of their
lives—a touch with the outside world and, above all, a sym-
pathetic understanding, so that the little delicacies we leave
are acceptable as gifts and not as a donation from patronizing
gringo travelers.

So when we decided to explore the plateau of the Sierra de
Juárez and I telephoned Ricardo to see if he could get a couple of real good, dependable men who could drive cars and
help with the camp work, Ricardo suggested that we employ
his woodcutter, Macario Montoya, and his handyman, Marcos
Romero.

The Sierra de Juárez form a high barrier between the rich
irrigated lands of the country south of Mexicali and the coast
to the south of Tijuana.

Directly to the east of the mountains, however, and before
coming to the irrigated plains, lies the desert of Laguna
Salada.

Marcos Romero, "The Big Gorilla," right, and Macario Montoya un-
loading the camp.

On the east, the Sierra de Juárez plunge precipitously into canyons. But on the west the slope is more gradual; and along the top is a huge plateau—four or five thousand feet above sea level—covered with beautiful timber interspersed with great piles of fractured granite.

Here also is the Laguna Hanson, a beautiful lake fed by a series of springs, bordered by pine trees.

Of the tourists who go to Tijuana and perhaps down to Ensenada there is not one in a hundred thousand who knows anything at all about this beautiful country. In fact, it is virtually terra incognita except to the woodchoppers.

I have previously mentioned the need for firewood in Mexican homes. There is also a need for fence posts to build the barbwire fences which are now taking the place of rock walls throughout much of Mexico. But for the visiting gringo in search of good food, the ribbonwood used for barbecuing is of personal concern.

For instance, there is something about the food in Ricardo Castillo's restaurant which is indescribable. It has a flavor

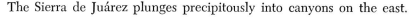

The Sierra de Juárez plunges precipitously into canyons on the east.

Pine trees border Laguna Hanson.

redolent of careful barbecuing and is similar to that of food cooked over the coals of a campfire in the open.

Part of the secret of this, of course, is good cooking. But a large part of the secret is the fact that Ricardo and his brother, Oswaldo, will not compromise on quality by permitting their meats to be cooked over a gas flame. Meats have to be carefully prepared over a wood fire, and not just any old type of wood will suffice. They use what they call ribbonwood, which is what we refer to as redshank. It is a first cousin to the manzanita. It is difficult to come by, and it has a very distinctive burning pattern. It makes coals which hold the heat with great tenacity and which impart a delicious flavor to meat cooked over them.

Getting sufficient quantities of redshank to keep a barbecue fire going twenty-four hours a day is something of a problem and Ricardo employs woodcutters who range out through the timber country, traveling many, many miles in order to bring in the necessary quantities of wood.

Chickens, beef, and pork being barbecued over hardwood coals.

One of these woodcutters is a very interesting individual named Macario Montoya.

Macario, the woodcutter, was familiar with all of the criss-cross roads which have been made by woodcutters along the plateau region and which would drive an ordinary tourist into nervous prostration, since many of these side roads are much better traveled than the so-called main road.

Moreover, Macario had, on one of his recent trips, stumbled upon a cave which had been lived in by ancient Indians and apparently had been left just as it had been for several hundred years.

In this cave was a perfect *olla*, completely intact, just as it had been last used by the ancient Indians. The mere fact of its presence and the fact that it was intact showed that no one had ever found the cave since the last occupant ceased to have any use for it.

There may have been skeletons in the cave, or other Indian artifacts. Macario didn't know. He was busy chopping wood, but he had seen the *olla* and knew that Ricardo would like to have it for an exhibit in the restaurant. So, he had picked up the *olla* and brought it along.

It may be mentioned here parenthetically that Ricardo and Oswaldo are fixing their restaurant so that it is not only a fine place in which to eat but is a place where the tourist who wants to go farther south can pick up a great deal of information about Baja California. They have road maps, photographs, and a great deal of first-hand information about the country.

The second helper, Marcos Romero, goes by the nickname of Gorilón, meaning the big gorilla.

One look at Marcos, and one knows how he got the nickname.

Since we were to leave at daylight on a Monday morning, Ricardo drove up to the ranch with the two helpers late Sunday afternoon.

Marcos, the big gorilla, was wearing a coat which had been split on the right side where the top of the sleeve joins the back.

Ricardo took me to one side to explain that Marcos was very much embarrassed. It was a brand-new coat, but they just don't make coats which will fit Marcos' framework. The huge muscles of the man's back and shoulders, the great neck, would baffle even a custom tailor. No matter how big Marcos tries to get his clothes, when he forgets and starts to lift something without taking his coat off first, the muscles swell, and something is going to rip.

Later on on the trip, when I found out what a perfect jewel of an individual Marcos was, I suggested to Ricardo that since he seemed embarrassed at the rip down the back of the coat I would buy him a new coat when we got back to Tijuana.

Ricardo simply smiled. "It won't do any good," he said. "Within two days that coat would be the same as this one. It happens every time he buys clothes."

"The Big Gorilla" is too powerful for his clothes.

Roscoe "Pappy" Hazard also was to go on this trip with us; and again he had insisted on buying the meat because, he explained, he had "contacts" in San Diego from whom he got good meat.

And contacts Pappy certainly has. I sometimes think he either owns half of San Diego or is on terms of intimate friendship with the men who do own half of San Diego. Pappy gets just about anything that is needed on a camping trip—except, perhaps, a new deck of cards. Since he plays constantly, a new deck of cards is almost certain to be well-worn at the expiration of a day or two.

So we sat around my ranch that evening building air castles, laying plans and making jokes, with Macario and Marcos, the big gorilla, being observantly silent.

8

A Futile Search

We had made arrangements to meet at Pappy Hazard's office and yard in San Diego at seven o'clock in the morning.

What we had failed to take into consideration at the time we made the plans was that this was the last Sunday in April, this was the day we set clocks ahead to Daylight Saving Time, so we lost an hour out of a night's sleep.

By the time this dawned on us it was too late to get in touch with Pappy to change plans and, what the heck, it meant getting up only an hour earlier; so, since we had said seven o'clock, we'd be there at seven o'clock. The only thing we wondered about was whether Pappy would remember that we were on a new time schedule Monday morning.

Pappy Hazard has an office and a yard there in San Diego that is absolutely unique.

Pappy's office has perhaps had more millions of dollars' worth of business stream through it than any office in San Diego and Pappy has a gift of inspiring loyalty in his employees; and his sons have the gift of giving men a chance to develop to the best of their capacity. They are wonderful executives in the real sense of the word. If I were a young

In Pappy Hazard's yard, getting ready to take off.

Pappy Hazard has a collection of animals from all over the world.

Interior of Pappy Hazard's private museum.

man with confidence in my own ability to develop, I think getting a job with that Hazard organization would be my goal for a first stepping stone.

Bruce Hazard, in particular, is one of the most interesting men I know. He gambles with contracts just as Pappy likes to gamble at poker—and just as it's nearly impossible to beat Pappy Hazard at poker, so is it almost impossible to beat Bruce at the contracting game.

The interesting thing at Pappy's yard and office, however, is that Pappy has fenced off a few hundred thousand dollars' worth of San Diego real estate for a feeding ground in which he has animals from all over the world. He has Texas longhorn cattle. He has llamas from South America. He has buffalo, bighorn sheep—you name it, he has it.

Then Pappy has his museum, a great, long building housing

relics of the Old West, and of a bygone era. Stagecoaches, buggies, surreys, wagons.

Some of these surreys are famous because they were owned by very wealthy, very prominent people back in the eighteen-hundreds.

Now, a century later, after the people who used them are dead and gone, after the economy of transportation has changed so that the horse and buggy has become an anachronism, Pappy has these priceless relics in his museum.

Because I always prefer to wait for the other man rather than have the other man wait for me, we arrived about twenty minutes early. But despite the fact it was the first day of Daylight Saving, despite the fact we were early, there were Pappy and Jack Trammel at the yard waiting.

We joined forces, drove across the border to Tijuana, and to Ricardo's restaurant, where a really sumptuous breakfast was awaiting.

We were joined at breakfast by Wulfrano Ruiz, who had tentatively planned to go along on the trip, but who had had

Pappy Hazard with some of his old-time wagons.

Ricardo Castillo, Wulfrano Ruiz, the Author, and Peggy Downs in front of Ruiz' mansion.

to cancel his plans at the last minute in order to be a good samaritan to an American friend (who was in all sorts of trouble because he had ignored many of the Mexican laws in trying to do business in Mexico).

Wulfrano Ruiz is a builder. He wants to build, build, build. He likes to build buildings. He likes to build human relationships. He likes to build international understanding. He is mentally alert. He has a wonderful sense of humor, and it was a blow to him that he couldn't join us on this trip. However, he had a job to do and he intended to do it to the best of his ability. So he shook hands and wished us the best of luck and settled down for a bite of breakfast with us.

Some day I am going to tell the whole story of Wulfrano Ruiz. It is one of the most inspirational stories I know.

Ruiz came from a relatively poor family, and, in Mexico, that means starting with a terrific handicap. But Ruiz was an observant youngster and a terrific worker. He saved money to

On the outskirts of Tijuana when it was erected, the palatial residence of Wulfrano Ruiz (the semicircular building in the center of the photograph) is now surrounded by the rapidly growing city.

buy a bicycle, and then decided he could rent his bicycle when he was not using it. So he rented the bicycle by the hour and with the money purchased other bicycles. All this, mind you, from a kid not yet ten years old.

By the time Wulfrano Ruiz was eight years old he was also running a little store selling certain staples at a profit.

Today Ruiz is one of Mexico's important citizens. His mansion in Tijuana is a palatial home which he built on what was then the outskirts of Tijuana. Now the city has grown to a point where traffic flows around his place in a never-ceasing stream. Yet, with the true Mexican love of privacy, Ruiz maintains his house and extensive patio as a restful island in the midst of all this bustling activity.

Ruiz has fitted up an office in his home for my use so that if

I wish to do writing or simply to take a siesta when I come to Tijuana, I have a luxurious room and bath at my disposal. And this is typical of the Mexican attitude, where friendships are the big things in life.

He has a clarity of vision which makes it a privilege to enjoy his friendship and listen to his conversation—and when a friend gets into trouble, Ruiz is not one to turn his back. So, when his American friend was in trouble, we knew we couldn't have the pleasure of enjoying Ruiz' company on our trip. Ruiz wanted very much to go, but friendship came first.

Eventually we finished breakfast, feeling that we wouldn't want to eat again for a week, and took off for Tecate.

It had been our plan to stock up with liquor at Tijuana, because it is too complicated to buy liquor on the American side and transport it across the border—just as it is impossible to buy liquor on the Mexican side and transport it back to California.

However, once more the calendar had crossed us up.

This was Labor Day in Mexico and everything was closed.

Ruiz took us out to his magnificent four-story mansion, took us down to his wine cellar, and insisted on giving us liquor for the trip—bottles of rare wine, rum that was fifty years old. In vain we protested; he simply pushed the bottles into our hands.

So we took off for Tecate, to find that here again we ran into parades, celebrations, bands, speeches, and holiday festivities.

We worked our way slowly through Tecate, then on through the foothill country up the grades until finally we came to La Rumorosa, where we were able to secure a few last-minute staples. Then we backtracked a couple of miles to where the road turned off to the south. And within a very short time we were in the midst of thousands of acres of beautiful plateau scenery.

A parade in Tecate.

Beautiful plateau country.

Ricardo Castillo, Macario, and Sam Hicks hold a conference.

The mountains are basically granite, with little plateaus in between the granite upthrusts where soil has accumulated and trees have grown up over the countless years.

This country is a national park, but the government permits the cutting of any dead timber. Therefore, the woodcutters have made roads crisscrossing the plateau region, bringing out truckload after truckload of dead wood.

Somewhere in this network of roads is a main road, and here or there one will encounter a road sign. But, for the most part, one must really know the country in order not to get lost.

We wanted, if possible, to take a look at the cave in which Macario had found the *olla,* and Macario felt that he could take us to it without any trouble. There was, he explained, a little mountain which looked exactly like the breast of an

Indian maiden; it rounded gently to the top, where there was a rock crown.

Macario had little trouble locating this really intriguing landmark, but from there on he had nothing but trouble.

He found the camp he had made when he had taken out seventeen loads of wood. He could remember all about the wood and all about the camp, because that was what he had been interested in primarily. The cave, however, had been

We make camp in the plateau country.

simply something that he had seen on the side and, while he had picked up the *olla* because he thought Ricardo would be interested in it, he had made no attempt to remember the exact location of the cave.

Here there were occasional upthrusts of granite interspersed among the trees; and from time to time Macario would indicate one of these granite upthrusts with an air of positive assurance, only later to admit defeat.

The exasperating thing was that we must have been within a few hundred feet of the cave on several occasions.

Macario said there were paintings in the cave. He had noticed these but hadn't paid enough attention to them to be able to describe them in detail.

So, finally, after a couple of hours spent in vain exploration we decided to make camp. We moved on down the road to the south several miles before finding just the place we wanted—where we could pull off the road, lose ourselves in the timber, build a campfire, put out our folding tables and chairs, and relax.

It had been a cold spring, and May had come in something like March—with a cold wind, which up here, at an elevation of four to five thousand feet, really had an edge to it. However, we had a cheery campfire, and Pappy had again purchased enough thick steaks to feed an army.

So we had a wonderful supper, relaxed for a while around the campfire, gave Pappy a few hands of penny ante to keep him happy, and then rolled into bed and deep, dreamless slumber—so much at variance with our sleep the night before, when I had been waiting for the alarm clock to go off, doing all my last-minute packing, and trying to pour a few words of hurried instructions into the dictating machine.

9

El Alamo

Morning in camp is a wonderfully stimulating sensation, particularly if it is in a cold, bracing climate.

The climate up there—at about five thousand feet above sea level—on this May morning was cool and crisp.

My sleeping bag was warm and comfortable. I snuggled down into it and appreciated Emerson's essay on compensation. The fact that I was no longer young was a handicap; but on the other hand, at my age nothing was expected of me; so I could lie there and let the others brave the experience of falling out of a warm sleeping bag into chill air some fifteen or twenty minutes before sunrise.

I heard the sound of an ax on wood. I saw the ruddy reflection of flames from the tree trunks. I heard the morning salutations as the men got up.

There is something about the Mexican habit of saying *"Buenos días"* to each member of the party that is heartwarming.

Gradually the light grew stronger. Soon the first rays of the sun turned the tops of the pine trees to molten gold. Then came the crackle of bacon cooking on a griddle over coals.

Sam Hicks whips up hotcake batter for breakfast.

The sound of Sam's big spoon as he whipped up a mess of *"tortillas gringas"* (hotcakes). Then the aroma of coffee. And I knew the time had come when I couldn't put off getting up any longer.

So I pulled down the zipper on the sleeping bag, took a deep breath, braced myself, and emerged into the crisp air, reaching for my clothes.

By the time I was dressed, Sam had breakfast ready. And, after ice-cold fruit juice, I had coffee, sausage, bacon, hotcakes, and then yielded to temptation and had a small piece of the barbecued meat that had been warmed up from the night before.

It was really a satisfactory breakfast.

As soon as breakfast was over the men started moving with that coordinated efficiency which is shared by first-class mili-

Sam Hicks, extreme right, sets a rapid pace in camp.

tary operations and by veteran campers who are getting camp
ready for the road.

It was a pleasure to watch these men do the job.

Dishes were washed and stored in boxes. Food was placed
in the refrigerator or in our iceboxes. Bedrolls were roped and
deposited in a pile. Folding chairs were collapsed and placed
ready for loading. Then these men, all of them big and powerful, started to toss the heavy bedrolls into the pickup and to
put loaded boxes of dishes, groceries, and perishables into the
camper.

I checked my cameras and coats in the Jeep Wagoneer
stationwagon, and, within a surprisingly short time, we were
ready for the road.

This mountain country is simply beautiful. The air is crystal clear and bracing. There are juniper trees and pine trees

growing in profusion. The dirt roads require reasonably careful driving, but since they are in country where the foundation
is largely decomposed granite, they are relatively good for
dirt roads, and very good indeed for Baja California roads.

Some forty-five-odd miles south of La Rumorosa is Laguna
Hanson, a beautiful mountain lake with trees running down
to the edge of the water. A few short miles below this lake is
the sawmill where a great deal of lumber is processed and
moved by trucks out of the mountains, down into the valley,
and then into Ensenada.

Jack Trammel, lower right, surveys the rugged mountain scenery on
the plateau.

A clear mountain lake with trees running to the edge of the water.

It is possible to get gasoline here at the lumber company. And here the motorist with a pickup, a four-wheel-drive car, or perhaps even a good car with unusually high clearance, can have a choice of several roads.

We wanted to see the old mining city of El Alamo, so we took off on the road which brought us down to the southern end of the Sierras. At first we dropped down out of the pine and juniper trees into oaks, and then into a rolling type of country well covered with high brush.

It was a long trip to El Alamo, the almost deserted mining camp, but when we arrived we felt the trip had been well worth while. Here was a wonderful ghost town. The mine had evidently been closed for years, and the town had been in the process of dying for some time, but here and there little spots of life were still hanging on persistently. There was a store

Ruined buildings at El Alamo.

which had its meager supplies replenished from time to time and which sold a few staples to the surrounding country. But the atmosphere of the place was dominated by buildings which were in a state of complete disrepair. A person interested in these old mining camps could spend a lot of time in El Alamo, rummaging among the old machinery, the decaying buildings, finding souvenirs of the old-time mining camp which, in its heyday, had been a beehive of prosperous activity.

As it was getting late, we had to make a brief exploration to find a suitable camp spot for the night.

Down there the country was quite flat, and we abandoned the main road in order to head for a group of trees which we saw a couple of miles away.

We had just established ourselves nicely in camp when the

Ricardo Castillo and Sam Hicks give the owner of the ranch an ice-
cold can of beer.

owner of the land came riding by on a very good-looking
horse. He welcomed us to his ranch with the typical hospitality of the Baja California rancher. And we, in turn, helped
him on his journey to his headquarters by giving him a cold
beer which, as it turned out, was very welcome, the day having turned quite warm in the afternoon down there in the
lower levels.

Again we had some of Pappy's choice Grade A meat, barbecued to the pink of perfection. Again we had enough poker
to give us something to talk about and something to laugh
about. And then once more we were wrapped in deep slumber
while overhead the stars seemed to move ever closer, the hush
of night fell over the country, and the crystal-clear air and the
silence furnished a benediction.

10

Interesting Characters

The Mission of Santa Catarina is the headquarters of the reservation of the PaiPai Indians.

It took us some time, however, to find the right road to the Mission Santa Catarina and, as subsequent events proved, we had been going pretty much around our elbow to get to our thumb.

However, the trip was interesting. At one point we came upon a dobe building which was on the verge of coming apart. One wall had pretty much separated from the others and was held in place by heavy wooden braces which had been thrust into the ground and slanted over so as to prop up the wall.

A woman came out at the sound of our motors, a woman perhaps in her late sixties. There was the usual quota of children, evidently her children and grandchildren.

We asked her about the road and received a very courteous answer. Then Ricardo, who has powers of quick observation, began to question her about more personal matters.

As Ricardo explained afterward, he saw that what few crops they were trying to grow had been irrigated by someone

The woman tells about her troubles.

carrying water in a bucket from a well and, of late, the ground had become parched.

Under Ricardo's questioning it turned out that the woman's husband was no longer young, that he was crippled with rheumatism and with some trouble which had caused one of his legs to swell, that he couldn't get out of bed, and that the woman was hoping to get some medicine which would help.

The only way she could accomplish this was to ask a friend to try to get medicine at Ensenada. But since this friend had no automobile he had to hitchhike to Ensenada; and since travel over the road was only haphazard, averaging perhaps one car a day in each direction, the prospects were not bright. The friend had started on his mission of mercy the day before. He might make the round trip in three days. It might take a week.

I had quite a medicine kit in my bags, but I was afraid to prescribe without knowing about the patient and, particularly, whether he might have an allergy to some of the medicines which we consider almost household remedies. It frequently happens that some analgesic which is taken as a matter of course by people who have accustomed themselves to its use will have rather serious side effects on people who perhaps have never had a dose of medicine in all their lives.

Ricardo asked her about food.

The woman said they had none.

He asked her about money.

Again she said they had none.

She asked us if we wanted to come in to talk with her husband, so Ricardo and I entered the house.

It was a typical dobe house with a dirt floor, but the beds were neatly made, and there was a general homey atmosphere about the place.

From the ceiling hung the foreleg and the head of an animal which I think was probably a deer. Every scrap of meat had been scraped from these bones except for a very few slivers remaining around the muscles of the head.

For some time now they had apparently been subsisting on nothing but meat. And now, with the head of the house laid up, it was impossible to get even that.

These people were hungry.

We had unfortunately packed our load so that all of our supplies, with the exception of the food we had left out for our lunch, were pretty well buried.

So we raided that and gave the woman apples, oranges, canned soup, and a loaf of bread.

A few miles down the road I began to kick myself. The way the packs were loaded, it would have taken half an hour or so to have broken into them, but if we had taken that half hour we could have given her a lot more groceries.

We had given her a little money, and with that money it

Only mounds of dirt from the decayed adobe walls mark the place where the Mission of Santa Catarina once stood.

would be possible for her to buy a few staples at the store at El Alamo, enough perhaps to last her for a week.

We kept on until we came to the headquarters of the PaiPai at Santa Catarina. Here we stopped and visited and looked over the ruins of the mission.

The dobe walls have now crumbled so that where the mission once stood, with its thick adobe walls and graceful arches, there is now nothing but a few little hills suggestive of the fact that there had at one time been walls here.

The PaiPai headquarters at Santa Catarina had been the scene of some interesting localized earthquakes some years earlier. The Indians told us that every day for a month the ground had moved and numerous hot springs were opened up.

Perhaps it is for this reason that the PaiPai dwellings are braced, wherever possible, by being anchored to huge rocks.

These Indians are superb horsemen and manufacture rawhide ropes and hair ropes.

These hair ropes are made by taking horsehair from the mane and tail, twisting it together, and then braiding it. The twisting and braiding is done by tying the first strands of the rope to a piece of wood, which is then rotated rapidly on a swivel. The ropemaker can whirl this wooden blade around the spindle with bewildering speed.

We asked some of these PaiPai Indians about the friends we had made earlier on the east slope of the mountains, and they all seemed to know Juan Arballo very well indeed. The man seemed to get around to all of the PaiPai country.

Later on, when we went some three or four miles to the general store which supplied the reservation, there was Juan Arballo as big as life, glad to see us, courteous, dignified, cordial, and as casual as if we had just left him a few hours ago at the adjoining ranch.

He was many miles from his home camp, and those were rough, mountainous miles; but he evidently thought nothing

Huge granite boulders brace the houses of PaiPai Indians against "the earth which moves."

Detailed view of the construction of a PaiPai house.

of walking long distances over rough terrain. He greeted us quite matter-of-factly.

We visited with him for a while and bought a little merchandise at the store, getting some frijoles in individual paper sacks so that in the future, whenever we came upon a family in need, we would be able to reach inside the camper and pull

Juan Arballo, courteous, dignified, and cordial.

out frijoles without going to the trouble of unpacking a lot of overburden.

We wanted to explore all of the road between El Alamo and San Felipe. Perhaps I should say all of the roads—plural —because there were many, and we had to feel our way, quite frequently getting on the wrong road.

However, we made camp that night in a beautiful valley where there were so many quail that I could hardly believe my eyes.

It has been many years since I have seen quail get up in such numbers that it is impossible for them to fly in a straight line; but here the numbers were such that in order to build up speed and avoid collision they had to fan out into a huge semicircle.

The next day we were up early and left Marcos, the big gorilla, and Macario to keep camp while Sam, Pappy Hazard, Ricardo, Jack Trammel, and I took the Ford pickup and the

Looking down on the desert country.

Jeep Wagoneer in which to make the long drive to San Felipe.

Shortly after we left camp we dropped down off from the mesa country into Valle Trinidad, where there were quite a few little ranches and where evidently an attempt is being made to develop water on a fairly large scale.

Then we dropped down again into a desert country where we found ocotillo, various types of cacti, and the typical desert verde trees mixed with thickets of mesquite—a beautiful but somewhat sandy desert country.

We reached San Felipe shortly after noon.

San Felipe is a fishing village and a sportsman's resort.

When the fishing is good, business is very good indeed in San Felipe. When the fishing is poor, business is very bad.

At the time of our arrival fishing had been bad. The weather had been chilly and windy. The water had been cold, and the tourist fishermen had been staying home in great numbers.

Left to right: Roscoe Hazard, Arnoldo Hellin, Gildardo Martínez, the Author, Miguel García, and Jack Trammel outside Arnold's Restaurant.

However, San Felipe is a beautiful little city, and we were soon renewing old acquaintances: Greeting Armando Vásquez, who is now running a sporting-goods store; going to Arnold's restaurant for lunch, eating freshly caught fish while we sat in a new addition looking out over the deep blue of the bay.

Then we went to the really well-stocked curio store for some leather goods and, for the first time, we were able to get what liquor we needed. At the San Felipe Liquor Store there is one of the smartest bilingual young women in all of Baja California, a young woman with a good sense of humor, a chain-lightning mind, a quick repartee, and a knowledge of how to deal with the public.

We bought some of the distinctive Mexican rolls and some *pan dulce* at the bake shop, picked up a few corn tortillas at

"The Big Gorilla" and Macario were left in camp.

the tortilla factory, took a few pictures, and managed to get back to camp an hour or so before dark.*

We had left Marcos and Macario with a deck of cards, all of the small change we had in camp, and, in addition, I had staked each one to two dollars in paper money. We left them with instructions to see who was the best card player.

It had evidently been quite a day for the two men, who are hardly accustomed to drawing wages for such a congenial occupation.

The next morning we were off to an early start and retraced

* Since this visit to San Felipe the place has been visited by a *chubasco*, one of the tropical storms which at times devastate the peninsula of Baja California. The terrific wind swept fishing boats into a tangled mass of wreckage, then drove them high up onto the beach. Torrential rains flooded the town—but the inhabitants were soon digging out and starting the staggering job of cleaning up.

The twelve-year-old boy who had charge of the ranch.

our way to the Mission of Santa Catarina and the PaiPai headquarters.

We had one notable experience, when we stopped at a ranch for directions and found that there was a shortcut we could take which would literally save miles.

The information was given us by one of the brightest twelve-year-old boys one could ever hope to encounter.

This young lad rattled off the information we wanted concisely, completely, and accurately.

Responsibilities had given the boy a remarkable maturity.

He seemed to be alone at the ranch, so I asked Ricardo to make inquiries.

The story was certainly curious.

This twelve-year-old boy was in charge of the ranch. His mother worked at a ranch some miles away, and I gathered that he saw her only at intervals. From time to time, he received provisions from the man who was, in turn, the representative of the owner of the ranch. It had been three months since this man had paid his last visit.

This twelve-year-old boy and his dog were living there perfectly content, wonderfully competent, and very much on the job.

I asked Ricardo to inquire what the boy lived on.

The answer came back quick as a flash, and everyone started to laugh. So I asked Ricardo to translate.

Ricardo said the answer was simply, "Miracles—we live on miracles."

The boy had a .22 rifle and apparently managed to get enough rabbits to keep himself and his dog supplied with meat.

The complete self-reliance of this young man, his alert mind, his quick-witted replies, his bearing, all created a tremendous impression.

It seems a shame that there are not more economic opportunities for men of that caliber in Baja California; but I think it is inevitable that this young man will drift to Tijuana, since he had evidently spent several years there; and I know that if he ever needs a job in Tijuana, Ricardo will put him to work and give him a chance to develop his talents.

We made a second stop at the Mission of Santa Catarina, found the road which went to the north and which was east of the road we had previously taken, and started our return trip —once more climbing up the slopes of the Sierra de Juárez.

After some fifteen miles we came to a ranch and pulled in to talk with the people who lived there.

Sauntering out to meet us was our friend, Juan Arballo, the PaiPai Indian.

These people at the ranch were, he explained, relatives of his. The men had all gone out to round up cattle, so Juan had gone up to keep the ranch going while the younger men were out riding.

We asked him how he had made the journey.

His answer was as simple as the means of transportation. He had walked.

He seemed mildly surprised that we would have asked the question—what other means of transportation was available to a PaiPai Indian who had no automobile?

We visited at the ranch for some time and really enjoyed ourselves. Then we moved on up the road until again we came to the forks just below the sawmill. Then we backtracked over some of the road we had taken a few days earlier

Juan Arballo was there to meet us.

until we came to a valley at the southwestern slope of the mountains; here we again turned north, this time to go along the western slope of the Sierra de Juárez.

After a few miles we came to a valley with a rushing stream of clear mountain water, huge live-oak trees to furnish shade, and level grassy meadows offering an ideal camping place.

So we camped fairly early and sat around the campfire, stretching out in comfortable chairs, relaxing, and talking about the trip.

The next day we were up early and, after some thirty miles, came to a most interesting ranch house where the family was glad to see us; but the father of the children was out hunting. So it was decided to send out to ask him to come in and visit with us.

There was a huge horse in the yard, and one of the boys

We camp by a mountain stream.

threw a saddle on him; then they took a little four-year-old boy and boosted him up into the saddle.

Heaven knows how tall that horse was. He was so tall that I don't think I could have got my left foot up high enough to reach the stirrup. But this little four-year-old kid, whose legs were so short that they seemed to stick straight out from his body when spread apart by the saddle, grabbed the reins, hit the horse a lick, and they started out looking for Daddy.

That horse understood the kid and the kid understood the horse.

The horse broke into a trot, and the kid stuck to that saddle like a burr.

They went down into the creek bottom, through the brush where rabbits might be expected to hang out and, sure enough, within a short time back they came, Daddy with his

The child seemed to understand the horse perfectly, and the horse certainly understood the child.

rifle and the kid perched as big as life atop the tall horse.

Then we brought out some beer, sat around and had cool refreshment, visiting and joking while Pappy—superb horseman that he is—climbed aboard a burro and Ricardo pulled himself up into the saddle of the tall horse.

It was quite apparent that the horse understood the four-year-old boy a lot better than he understood Ricardo. But with an air of complete boredom he let Ricardo put him through his paces. Then, after Ricardo had dismounted, the "big gorilla" climbed aboard, and a hilarious time was had by all of us.

After reluctantly leaving our newfound friends, we headed on north—and all of a sudden, almost before we knew it, in the distance we saw cars moving rapidly at right angles to our line of travel. Then we came to the paved road between Tecate and Mexicali, turned onto the pavement, and became a part of a stream of traffic.

In Tecate we went to a very fine Italian restaurant, seated ourselves at a table in civilized fashion, and had a great variety of dishes, skillfully cooked, wonderfully well served. And then we were across the border on the United States side, and before dark I was steaming in a hot shower at my ranch in Temecula.

That morning I had been camped far down in the Sierra de Juárez, in this beautiful little valley with its mountain stream rushing through it, the giant live-oaks casting a shade, the sun brilliant, the air crystal clear, where the country is wild and teeming with game. There, coveys of quail sounded like the beating of a snare drum, and the nights are punctuated by the shrill scream of the coyote. Yet within a few miles are the thriving cities of Ensenada and Tijuana on the west, the state capital of Mexicali and the town of San Felipe on the east.

This Magic Square of northern Baja California has perhaps the greatest variety of people and scenery of any area of comparable size anywhere in the world—a primitive country close to our own doors.

I was immersed in this primitive, simple life early in the morning. Nine hours later I was at my desk in my office in Temecula, surrounded by dictating machines and an accumulated pile of urgent matters demanding attention.

Yet always in my mind was the thought of a return trip and the courageous little old woman whose husband was lying there on the bed, who had no food and no money.

Ricardo had felt the same way. And Ricardo had suggested that we take our Grasshoppers, which are designed to go at high speed over rough roads, drive to Ensenada, make the trip out to this house with an ample stock of provisions, and return to Ensenada in one day.

Hotcakes and bacon cooking over a bed of coals.

The trip would be rough and rugged. We had only three Grasshoppers we could take on the trip; but the men seemed to feel that the Jeep Wagoneer could be used as an auxiliary car without slowing down the caravan.

Then the phone rang and a new adventure opened up.

A Mexican laborer had found a figurine, possibly of historic interest, near a cave in the environs of San Felipe. We would have to investigate that too.

So, before we knew it, I was rushing through the most urgent of my affairs. J. W. Black was coming down from Paradise. Wulfrano Ruiz felt that he could get away long enough to go on the trip and was anxious to accompany us. Oswaldo Castillo, Ricardo's brother, couldn't get away for a long trip when Ricardo was absent but was anxious to join us for this trip.

Suddenly we realized we had all of our vehicles jammed to capacity. Everyone was keen for this new adventure as well as our errand of mercy.

11

The Figurine

Some of the great pleasures of an expedition to the wild parts of Baja California are anticipation, preparation, and having the sheer fun of getting together.

The *National Geographic Magazine* had recently sent an expedition down to Baja California for a comprehensive coverage, and J. W. Black had been along on that trip with one of his Grasshoppers. Quite naturally, Sam Hicks, Jean Bethell, and I had been tremendously interested in where the expedition had gone, what it had found, etc., etc.; and that Sunday night when J. W. Black arrived at the ranch, he was full of information and gossip.

We sat around over cooling drinks, listening and talking, and Black had an almost incredible story, the story of the dog named Tonto.

Readers who are familiar with my book, *Off the Beaten Track in Baja,*will remember the story of Tonto, the big dog of uncertain breed who had evidently tried to follow his master's car for many, many miles until he had worn the pads off

* William Morrow & Company, Inc., 1967.

Left to right: Alfonso Martínez, Ricardo Castillo, Wulfrano Ruiz, Capitán Francisco Muñoz, the Author, Amy Muñoz, and Sra. María Elena Zepeda.

his feet so that he could hardly stand up, who was so ravenously hungry that if we poured bacon grease out on the sand, Tonto would eagerly gulp down sand and all.

We had kept Tonto in our camp for three or four days, and then we had arranged to see that he had a home in Santa Rosalía.

J. W. Black told us that now, more than a year later, he and Bruce Barron were walking down the street in Mulegé, some forty or fifty miles from the place where they had last seen Tonto, when suddenly they heard a bark and turned to see a great dog come charging toward them.

For a moment they were somewhat fearful, because there had been quite an outbreak of rabies in Baja California, and this dog certainly was pushing people to one side as he made a headlong rush toward them. Then the dog was on them and was all over them, whining, licking their hands, wagging his tail hysterically.

"Good Lord," Black said, "it's Tonto!"

And, at the sound of his name and the realization that he had been recognized, the dog went into another ecstasy of joy.

Black and Barron made inquiries and found the dog was indeed Tonto and that he now had a good home.

This certainly was a remarkable exhibition of canine intelligence and memory. Black and Barron had been but two persons in the camp, which at times had consisted of fifteen to nineteen people. The dog had seen them only a few days, yet he had remembered them, their scent, the sound of their voices, for more than a year.

How I wish that we could have taken Tonto north with us and given him a home at the Rancho del Paisano!

Black had lots of other gossip for us and we sat up quite late. But since we were going to have to get up at four o'clock in the morning to make a five o'clock start, we finally listened to reason and rolled in.

Four o'clock in the morning came very soon indeed, but we were ready to go despite the fact it was now four o'clock Daylight Saving Time.

We loaded our cameras, our duffels, drove to San Diego, then across the border to Tijuana, and went directly to Ricardo's restaurant, arriving there within one minute of our scheduled time of arrival.

Ricardo had breakfast ready.

Capitán Francisco Muñoz, the famous flier who has always done my charter flying south of the border, now owns a far-flung airline with valuable franchises, but he had set aside the

Left to right: Capitán Abraham Lechuga Pérez, Jean Bethell, Capitán Francisco Muñoz, Ricardo Castillo, and Wulfrano Ruiz, in front of Muñoz' plane.

day so he could fly us to San Felipe. He joined us for breakfast, and afterwards, we went to the airport where Capitán Muñoz had one of his Lodestars all ready to go.

Capitán Muñoz is a remarkable character, a flying genius, a man who can take big planes in and out of short airstrips where the average flier would face almost certain disaster.

How he does it is perhaps something of a secret.

Recently one of the aviation magazines assigned a flying expert to take a series of trips with Muñoz and describe in detail just how he manages to land and take off on those short strips.

The expert wrote a highly technical article in the magazine, the gist of which was that he couldn't believe what he had

seen; but he did include in his article some data he had col-
lected which, to his mind at least, cleared up the mystery part
of the thing. Nevertheless, it all seemed to boil down to saying, "It's perfectly feasible if you can only do certain things,
but Capitán Muñoz is the only one I have seen who can do
those things in exactly that way."

As far as I am concerned, Capitán Muñoz' technique can be
summed up in one word—experience.

Muñoz has to his credit some fifteen thousand hours of
flying time over some of the worst terrain in the world, terrain
where there are no aids to navigation, no emergency fields,
nothing but inhospitable jagged mountains, unexplored canyons, and an occasional oasis with a landing field and a
hotel.

Some time ago the Mexican Government presented Muñoz
with a gold medal representing an award for his having flown
over ten thousand hours with safety.

I have spent many hours in the air with Capitán Muñoz,

Capitán Muñoz, veteran pilot.

Ricardo Castillo, right, pulls a fast one on Capitán Muñoz.

some of it flying from point to point, some of it exploring, sometimes landing on improvised fields which we had made ourselves. At times there were no landing places at all— only a strip of beach or a piece of flat, weed-covered ground where only Muñoz' keen eyes could detect a safe shot with no rocks partially concealed by the weeds. Sometimes we have landed on rough dirt roads.

I don't know how he does it, and other aviators have told me they don't know how he does it, but it seems that Muñoz can fly anything anywhere anytime. And now that he has graduated into running scheduled airlines over Baja California, Muñoz really seems to have things coming his way.

However, the man who is now a busy airline executive never forgets the times when we were exploring Baja California together; he always tries to arrange his pressing responsibilities so that when I am taking a trip he can be with me at least a part of the time.

This time we were going to San Felipe to trace down the rumor about the carved figure. But, knowing from experience how infrequently these things pan out in real life, we also wanted to use the opportunity to explore the eastern escarpment of the Sierra de Juárez by getting views from the air.

The treasure part of the expedition was so highly hypothetical that it had to be considered as of sufficient importance to warrant an investigation, but not of sufficient importance to warrant any great excitement.

An uneducated but honest Mexican laborer, while hunting, had found a carved figurine near a cave. He was too superstitious to explore the cave, but he had taken the figurine to his home. He would be glad to let us see it, and, if we deemed it a significant find, he would take us to the place where he had found it.

His description of the figurine was such that it seemed reasonably certain it was not one of the crude clay figures which were made as dolls or idols by the early Indians.

The man insisted the little figure, which had been carved and polished, was that of a cow.

It was a story worth looking into—especially since it gave us an excuse for an air reconnaissance of that eastern escarpment.

The whole crowd was in a jovial mood as we left the airport at Tijuana, flew out over the exclusive residential district, then on east to Tecate, then over the plateau region at La Rumorosa, and finally over to where the paved highway winds down through the rugged mountains to the floor of the desert.

In order to fully appreciate the engineering that went into that road it is really necessary to see it from the air.

Looking down on the mountains one would feel that it would be a physical impossibility to get a road down those precipitous slopes to the desert below. Yet the road is not only

The high-class residential district of Tijuana.

there, it has been constructed with a constant grade, winding like some cement serpent through huge granite peaks, skirting deep canyons where even the surveying must have been precarious in the extreme.

We turned south and left the road, following along the edge of the high mountains.

When we had made our previous exploration by automobile, I had known that this was an untamed country, but I didn't realize how untamed it was until, sitting there in that airplane, I could see the tumbled mass of sheer mountains of the eastern escarpment.

There must be literally thousands of places in those mountains where human foot has never left a print, canyons known only to the *borrego* (mountain sheep) and kindred wildlife.

Over to the east, bordering Laguna Salada, we could see a

San Felipe from the air.

road; and from time to time, in some of the main canyons we caught glimpses of woodcutters' roads, or roads leading to ranches such as the road to the Dowling ranch, which we had explored. But, for the most part, there were no roads at all, no trails, nothing except a jumbled mass of wild terrain.

It was an awe-inspiring sight.

Some day I would like to return to this country with two, or perhaps three, helicopters and explore one or two of these canyons. It would be a hair-raising experience, one which would almost certainly land us in country which had never been explored by any human being. But it would be a terrific task to arrange for supplies in the main camp, gasoline, water, provisions, and perhaps shelter. Yet this wild, wild country is only a short airplane flight from the United States border.

We followed the eastern line of the mountains, then went

Friends greeting us in San Felipe.

over the PaiPai Indian country, and soon were scouting the field at San Felipe—a field which was theoretically too short for the *Lodestar*, but Muñoz, without batting an eyelash, took the big plane in with room to spare.

We were met by my friend Armando Vásquez and soon were joined by quite a crowd of people, many of whom we knew.

It took some time to locate the residence of the man who had found this carved figure near the cave.

Eventually, however, we located him and went to his house.

There were far too many of us. The man's modest place had never seen any such a delegation before, and our informant had the natural reaction which one would expect under the circumstances.

He was scared stiff.

The man who found the figurine.

It took us a long while to get anything at all out of him, and even then I was convinced that he was holding back. In fact, later on, and in a private conversation with Muñoz, he admitted that such had been the case.

In his first conversation with Muñoz he had very definitely described a cave near the place where he had found the little figure. There had been something about that cave which had indicated to his mind that it had been used by men who had landed in small boats and then gone to the cave. He also had either looked into this cave and seen a skeleton or in some other way had gotten the idea a dead man had been left in it.

It may be mentioned parenthetically that many of these caves in Baja do contain skeletons because the early Indians used them for burial.

I knew as soon as we talked with this man that we had

Figurine of the cow with the broken monkey clinging to its back.

moved in too quickly and in too great numbers. He sought refuge in becoming vague and indefinite.

However, there was one tangible thing he had said he possessed, and this we wanted to see—the carved figure which he had picked up, presumably near the cave.

For a while he seemed to me to want to evade the issue on that; but after a while, and under pressure of questioning, he produced the figure.

What was it? Where had it come from?

My own feeling is that this figure was made by a sophisticated craftsman. It may be five years old or it may be a hundred. It is some four inches long, two inches high, and three-quarters of an inch thick. It represents a cow lying down, with what evidently had been a monkey seated on its back—but the monkey has broken in two, so that only the lower half of the animal remains clinging to the cow's back.

It was carved from some sort of soft rock and was made flat on the bottom so that the little figure, when used perhaps as a table or shelf ornament, would sit upright. It could perhaps have been a modern ornament made somewhere in the Orient, sold as a curio, and then carried as a pocket piece or charm and lost.

Or conceivably, by one chance in a thousand, it might have been made by some highly gifted artisan of a bygone New World civilization.

We took pictures. We talked as best we could with the man, who was too frightened to really give us what information he had, and who perhaps didn't have as much information as he had wanted us to believe.

In short, as far as learning whether the cave contained any thing else of value, the trip could be considered only a preliminary step. We'll have to go back in the near future, when there are not so many of us, and take a lot more time digging out details—a fact here and another fact there. We will have to win the man's confidence and overcome his superstitious fear of disturbing a cave where, in all probability, he had seen a human skeleton, or bones which he assumed were human.

We had had a wonderful time. We had explored the eastern escarpment of the Sierra de Juárez from the air, and now we were going to have a savory fish luncheon at Arnold's.

We went to the restaurant, which had a patio opening out on the blue ocean with its tang of fresh salt air, and sat where

From the patio of Arnold's Restaurant, we recorded two huge sea bass that "didn't get away."

we could look out over waters (which were a deep indigo blue) and across a beach of dazzling white sand; and we watched fishermen bringing in their catches.

As we prepared to eat, a boat came in with a huge sea bass. We adjourned to take pictures. Then, back to the restaurant to eat lunch; then to the airplane, and off for Tijuana.

This time we flew over Santa Catarina and the PaiPai Indian Reservation, over the plateau land we had explored by automobile, and landed without incident at Tijuana; here we climbed into our automobiles and took off for Ensenada, arriving in time for dinner at the Hotel Bahía, and a beautifully executed Mexican floor show.

12

Errand of Mercy

The next morning we were up early. We loaded the Jeep Wagoneer with some luxuries and many necessities, flour, beans and lard, with many bags of candy.

We took off over the road to San Felipe, climbing through a beautiful mountain range where we followed a canyon up along a watercourse through the dense shade of towering oak trees; we passed prosperous little ranches, and continued on up to the little store at Ojos Negros, where we found that luxury of luxuries, a big refrigerator cooled by butane gas with ice-cold soda pop and beer.

Here we picked up a hitchhiker, a young man who was trying to get to his parents' ranch some distance down the road.

In the untraveled parts of Baja California one does not pass up hitchhikers, just as in the United States one who is at all careful should *never* pick up a hitchhiker, no matter how prepossessing he seems.

While we were on a traveled road which might have two or three cars a day, there are roads in Baja California where a

We paused beneath the welcome shade of huge live oaks.

man could wait for two or three days without seeing a single automobile.

So we loaded our lad aboard, despite the fact that visiting his ranch would require a little detour from our main line of travel, and moved on.

At the boy's ranch the family was wonderfully hospitable. They insisted that we partake of refreshments and sit in the shade for a while before moving on to El Alamo.

El Alamo is a ghost town, the site of the abandoned mine which I described earlier, and I believe there is opportunity for a lot of exploration in the vicinity.

J. W. Black, who is interested in anything mechanical, was in seventh heaven inspecting the old abandoned mining machinery and deducing when and where it had been manufactured, to what use it had been put, and how it had worked.

Our hitchhiker and his two sisters.

However, we were now traveling on a pretty tight schedule; so we pushed on to the ranch where the woman and children had been trying to operate with no food and no money, and with a sick husband who was laid up in bed.

Apparently someone had already come to their rescue, because the situation was entirely different now from what it had been when we were there before. The man of the house was up and around. The woman seemed much more cheerful. The children, who had just been rounding up a milk cow, returned with soda-pop bottles full of rich, fresh, creamy milk.

But they were certainly glad to get the provisions we had brought—and how their eyes lit up at the sight of the bags of candy!

They simply couldn't wait.

We found the man of the house up and around, the place stocked with food, the children happy—and delighted with candy we brought.

They took the candy, and with wide grins on their faces, kept talking and eating.

We had an idea the sweets might be bad for the man's arthritis or rheumatism, whatever it was; but after all, we had brought them enough provisions so they could coast along for quite some time; and it was nice to see this household, which had been faced with such deep gloom a short time before, now laughing and happy.

We had now explored every foot of the road between Ensenada and San Felipe, had camped in the plateau region of Sierra de Juárez, and explored the eastern escarpment from the air; and we had covered the dread desert bordering Laguna Salada and gone up the woodchoppers' roads and into the only canyons which had roads. We had seen the Pai-Pai Indians, and now all that remained was to get a little more data about Ensenada, Tijuana, and Mexicali—and we would have pretty well covered Mexico's Magic Square.

It was a long, hard trip back to Ensenada, but we arrived there shortly before dark; and Oswaldo, who was keenly conscious of his responsibilities in operating the restaurant during Ricardo's absence, insisted on taking off in one of the Grasshoppers to get to Tijuana that evening (over the new freeway which has been constructed between Ensenada and Tijuana, it is a matter of only little over an hour).

As far as we were concerned, however, we went to the hotel to explore the luxury of hot baths; then we went to the El Rey Sol Restaurant, where we had one of the most delightful dinners one could find anywhere.

We rolled into our beds, had a night of deep sleep, and the next morning visited some of the curio stores in Ensenada.

The store operated by the Chinese is really a remarkable place.

Our Grasshoppers ready for the long, hard trip to Ensenada.

The Author goes shopping in Ensenada.

For some years I had been trying to get a certain Chinese idol, and my searching had been rather purposeful. I had covered curio stores in San Francisco, in the Chinatown there, and in Los Angeles. For years I had asked my Chinese friends to be on the lookout and to buy such an idol if they found it, regardless of the cost.

My search had been fruitless.

But there in Ensenada I found a beautiful specimen of the idol that I wanted, a specimen carved with cunning skill from some tropical hardwood.

So eager was I to get this that I didn't take time to fully explore the wonderful stock of Oriental merchandise, nor did I have time to shop in some of the other stores.

No story of Mexico's Magic Square would be complete without commenting on the part which San Diego plays in all this.

13

San Diego

Just as we are inclined to take the two most essential things in life for granted—the air we breathe and the water we drink—so are the citizens of San Diego inclined to accept their wonderful climate and various civic attractions as a part of existence.

Situated on the water so that the climate is equable, with cool ocean breezes in summer, sunshine almost three hundred and sixty-five days a year, San Diego is a little section of Paradise.

In its own right, San Diego has tourist attractions which are unexcelled.

The San Diego Zoo is conceded to be just about the best in the world. Here are about a hundred broad, sunny acres with thirty-seven hundred animals kept as nearly as possible in their natural environment, with plenty of sunlight, fresh air and, above all, lots of room.

There is an absence of the crowded animal smells, the stench which so frequently characterizes the many zoos in cities where cages are placed beside each other in long rows.

Seeing the San Diego Zoo, wandering around through the

Entrance to San Diego Zoo.

Pachyderms . . .

sun-swept spaces, seeing animals that are quiet and contented, a person can have as much healthful exercise as he would get in a day of golf.

Or, if he prefers, he can mount one of the vehicles which makes a sweep around through the rolling terrain.

At Point Loma, the tourist will find himself standing on the most southwesterly point of land in the United States. Here is the old Spanish lighthouse, and a magnificent view stretches from the mountains back of Tijuana, over the city of San Diego, and then back to the east—where the mountains brood over the valley.

San Diego is literally filled with historic spots, old houses, old inns, old restaurants, the oldest brick structure of Southern California, the first mission to be founded in Southern California; and in a section known as Old Town, there are many historic restaurants which served Spanish food to the

. . . and bears.

The Author with two of the smiling waitresses at Castillo's Restaurant.

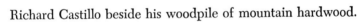

Richard Castillo beside his woodpile of mountain hardwood.

pioneers and which are still serving delicious Mexican food either within the restaurants or in patios under the shade of spreading trees.

In San Diego is moored the old sailing ship, *The Star of India,* which has been converted into a floating maritime museum.

The modern restaurants are of the best, serving distinctive dinners. In fact, San Diego enjoys the reputation of being a "good eating city."

But until recently San Diego has simply taken for granted one of the greatest assets it has—its proximity to Baja California.

The mathematics of the situation are interesting.

Some fifty-five thousand tourists cross the border to pour into Tijuana each day.

Left to right: Wulfrano Ruiz, Marshall Houts, Jean Bethell, Doug Allen, and Bob de Roos. Standing, Bob McCann.

Star of India docked at San Diego's Marine Museum.

It would certainly seem that these tourists should stop over in San Diego—in fact, that the tour of Tijuana should normally originate in San Diego.

However, a survey shows that the total number of rooms which San Diego can conjure up for transients is twenty-one thousand.

Even if the facilities of San Diego were fully occupied and even if fifty percent of the rooms had two people to a room, the plain, simple mathematics show that hundreds of thousands of dollars are escaping San Diego's coffers because the city isn't capitalizing sufficiently on the Mexican tourist trade.

And, as for Tijuana, it is an economic crime that the golden horde of tourists which daily pour into the city don't leave more money behind them.

There are a variety of reasons for this.

Lunching at Castillo's restaurant, left to right, Bob de Roos, Mrs. Maxwell, Dean Maxwell of U.C.L.A. Law School, Mrs. Houts, Sra. Ruiz, and the Author. Standing, Doug Allen.

Far too many people who go to Tijuana with money to spend don't spend it simply because they don't find anything to spend it on; and yet Tijuana, which is a free port, has some of the greatest bargains in the world.

Tijuana needs more shopping centers, more parking spaces, more advertising, and, above all, a better public image.

Tijuana is making giant strides forward under the administration of my friend, Mayor Francisco López Gutiérrez.

And San Diego, in a wonderful spirit of international friendship, is extending a helping hand.

Nowadays, the mayors of the two cities work together to give each other mutual assistance.

For some time, United States currency has circulated freely

The Author talks with Pat Branin, first Assistant to the Mayor of Ensenada.

south of the border. Any Tijuana or Ensenada merchant will gladly accept United States dollars at the current rate of exchange.

Until somewhat recently the reverse had not been true. That is, the San Diego merchant didn't want to accept the Mexican "peso" which, at the present time, has a value of approximately eight cents.

Recently, however, as a result of better coordination and understanding, the San Diego merchants decided that they would accept the peso in trade.

As soon as that happened, the merchants were astounded at the increased volume of business that they had from people who were living south of the border. Pesos poured in, in a veritable flood.

So now it is generally understood that the business life of the two cities is more closely united than had been considered

Looking from the blimp toward Tijuana and the stream of cars headed north.

to be the case a few years previously, and that a prosperous Tijuana means a prosperous San Diego.

It is refreshing to see the friendship and cooperation which is springing up between the two cities and the hands-across-the-border sentiment which is coming into existence.

More tourists pour into Tijuana each day than visit Las Vegas, and those Tijuana tourists have just as much money to spend. Las Vegas has glitter and charm, so tourists almost automatically stop over. Tijuana needs to be better understood.

There is no reason why Tijuana and San Diego couldn't reap a much greater harvest of the tourist dollar than is presently being diverted to their cash registers.

Recently we had a long talk with Patrick Branin, First Assistant to the Mayor of San Diego, and later on a letter from the Honorable Frank Curran.

FRANK CURRAN
MAYOR

March 19, 1968

Dear Mr. Gardner:

Your forthcoming book "Baja California's Magic Square" will be a major contribution to the growing understanding between people of upper and lower California and indeed of both nations.

I am particularly pleased to learn that your interest as a writer has been intrigued by the good relationship and cooperation between my City of San Diego and the City of Tijuana.

There are very significant depths to the joint efforts of both city administrators and private citizens in elevating the standards of living in the border areas and in long-range planning for improvements in public facilities such as highways, flood control, and parks which will be mutually shared for the benefit of all people.

Yours truly,
Frank Curran

Mr. Erle Stanley Gardner
P.O. Box 67
Rancho Del Paisano
Temecula, California

Both of these men are cooperating with Tijuana and are anxious to continue building the most cordial relations with Baja California. They are also becoming keenly conscious of the asset San Diego has because of its proximity to Tijuana and Ensenada.

Because we are inclined to be a self-sufficient people, we do not know the Mexicans well enough. When we go to their country, we think in terms of economic development rather than in terms of lasting friendships.

We should know more about the Mexicans, their cultural background, their loyalties to their friends, their standards of values, their concepts of the good things of life.

The time is coming when the various peoples of the world must learn to understand and respect each other, and Mexico is a mighty good place to begin.

Baja California is beautiful. As we have mentioned, the coast between Tijuana and Ensenada contains some of the

The Honorable Frank Curran, Mayor of San Diego.

Baja California is beautiful.

most picturesque ocean scenery in the world. The tourist who wants to get the most out of his vacation dollar can go to San Diego for a week; then he can go south of the border "down Mexico way" for four or five days and then return thrilled with a new experience, with colored slides or motion pictures which will captivate his friends, and with the knowledge that he has spent only a fraction of the money it would have cost him to take a vacation in any other foreign country.

It is to be borne in mind that in Mexico a laborer can live and live well on a wage which, at the current rate of exchange, is about four dollars in United States currency.

Travelers who are accustomed to going abroad where prices are sharply escalated for the tourist have an agreeable surprise when they go to Baja California.

People in search of a foreign vacation can find everything they want in Tijuana and Ensenada. There are splendid hotels. There are restaurants serving fine foods. There is an unequaled opportunity to purchase souvenirs and curios. There are all sorts of sightseeing, and boats which take out fishing parties, there are drives over good roads into beautiful back-country, and all of this virtually for peanuts.

In short, this Magic Square of Mexico is a delightfully complex area to explore. There is excellent fishing on both the East Coast at San Felipe and on the West Coast at Ensenada. In between there is some country which is virtually unknown. There is a desert with warm sunlight in the winter. There is a plateau country. There are cities.

And, above all, there are people who make wonderful friends.